MacCarthy ON CROSS-EXAMINATION

MacCarthy ON CROSS-EXAMINATION

TERENCE F. MACCARTHY

Cover design by ABA Publishing

Excerpt from *Presumed Innocent* by Scott Turow (Farrar, Straus & Giroux, 1987) used by permission of the author.

11 10 5 4

Library of Congress Cataloging-in-Publication Data
MacCarthy, Terence.
Maccarthy on cross-examination / Terence F. MacCarthy.
p. cm.
1. Cross-examination—United States. I. Title.
KF8920.M33 2007
347.73'75—dc22 2007026114

Discounts are available for books ordered in bulk. Special consideration is given to state bars, CLE programs, and other bar-related organizations. Inquire at Book Publishing, ABA Publishing, American Bar Association, 321 North Clark Street, Chicago, Illinois 60610.

www.ababooks.org

Epigraph

"The age-old tool for ferreting out truth in the trial process is the right to cross-examination. For two centuries past, the policy of the Anglo-American system of evidence has been to regard the necessity of testing by cross-examination as a vital feature of the law."

Perry v. Leake, 488 U.S. 272, 283 n.7 (1989)

"[T] he principal purpose of cross-examination [is] to challenge whether the declarant was sincerely telling what he believed to be the truth, whether the declarant accurately perceived and remembered the matter he related, and whether the declarant's intended meaning is adequately conveyed by the language he employed."

Ohio v. Roberts, 448 U.S. 56, 71 (1980)

"Cross-examination often depends for its effectiveness on the ability of course to punch holes in a witness, testimony at just the right time, in just the right way."

Perry v. Leake, 488 U.S. 272, 282 (1989)

The Sixth Amendment right of an accused to confront the witnesses against him is a "fundamental right."

Pointer v. State of Texas, 380 U.S. 400, 403 (1965).

"[A] denial of cross-examination without waiver . . . would be constitutional error of the first magnitude and no amount of showing of want of prejudice would cure it."

Brookhart v. Janis, 384 U.S. 1, 3 (1966)

In *Alford v. United States,* 282 U.S. 687, 692 (1931), in reversing a federal conviction because of restrictions on cross-examination, a unanimous Court stated:

> It is the essence of a fair trial that reasonable latitude be given the cross-examiner, even though he is unable to state to the court

> what facts a reasonable cross-examination might develop. Prejudice ensues from a denial of the opportunity to place the witness in his proper setting and put the weight of his testimony and his credibility to a test, without which the jury cannot fairly appraise them. . . . To say that prejudice can be established only by showing that the cross-examination, if pursued, would necessarily have brought out facts tending to discredit the testimony in chief, is to deny a substantial right and withdraw one of the safeguards essential to a fair trial.

And in *Smith v. Illinois*, 390 U.S. 129, 132-33 (1968), the Court reversed a state conviction where the trial judge restricted the right of cross-examination.

"Cross-examination is the greatest legal engine ever invented for the discovery of truth."

5 J. Wigmore, *Evidence* § 1367 (J. Chadbourn, rev. 1974)

"Cross-examination is the principle means by which the believability of a witness and the truth of his or her testimony are tested."

Davis v. Alaska, 415 U.S. 308, 316 (1974).

Contents

Acknowledgments

This book is dedicated to, in proper order, three groups of people.

First and obviously, my wonderful wife, Marian, who, because of her many years with me, is assured a place in heaven. Our children, who fortunately usually act like their mother: our eldest, Dan; Sean and his lovely wife, Micha; my namesake, Terry, and his wonderful wife, Aicha Marie; and our daughter, Megan, and her great husband, Tim O'Sullivan. Also our delightful and entertaining grandchildren, Kylee, Leah, Donal, Jude, and the twins, Deirdre and Dori. They keep me going.

Next, I thank all of the dedicated lawyers and supporting staff with whom I have had the privilege of working at our Federal Defender office. Also my fellow Federal Defenders and their committed lawyers and support staff, who are responsible for the finest defender services the world has ever known.

The third group (note my love for having three things) is as large as it is important.

Trial lawyers are indeed a special group. They profit much from the opportunity to work together and exchange ideas. They profit much from the comrades they enjoy. They profit much from their mutual love for what they do.

I have been blessed by the opportunity to work with and learn from many trial lawyers and judges. In appreciation, I dedicate this book to them.

Alaska:	Ray Brown
Arizona:	Russ Born, Bob Hirsch, Robert McWhirter, Jon Sands, Heather Williams
Arkansas:	William O. James, Jr.

California:	Marilyn Bednarski, Juanita Brooks, James J. Brosnahan, Judy Clarke, John Cleary, Brian Donato, David A. Elden, Jeff Hansen, Eugene Iredale, Rikki Klieman, Michael Pancer, Jon Minsloff, Marcia Morrissey, Phillip Pennypacker, Grover Porter, Judge Manuel Real, Dennis Roberts, Bart Sheela, Michael Stepanian, Barry Tarlow, Vicki Young, Howard L. Weitzman
Colorado:	Justice Michael Bender, Judge Russ Carparelli, Linda Miller, Steve Rench, Richard Tegtmeier, Craig Truman
District of Columbia:	Jud Best, Ken Curtis, Hays Gorey, Jr., Tom Horton, A. J. Kramer, John Lowe, Bill Moffitt, Steve Saltzburg, Mike Tigar
Florida:	Skipp Babb, Joe Beeler, Roy Black, Barry Cohen, Jim Gailey, Fred Haddad, Carey Haughwout, Richard Hersch, Milton Hirsch, Albert Krieger, Bruce Lyons, Tony Natale, Hugo Rodriguez, Judge E. J. Salcines, Teresa Sopp, Jeffrey Weiner, Fred Zinobar
Georgia:	Chris Adams, Tony Axam, Deryl Dantzler, Dennis De La Rue, Sam Dennis, Ed Garland, Jim Jenkins, Bobby Lee Cook
Hawaii:	Birney Bervar, Richard Turbin
Idaho:	John Adams, Jim Davis, Tim Gresback, Richard Rubin
Illinois:	Judge Marvin Aspen, Judge William Bauer, Carol Brook, John Buckley, Ken Cunniff, Tom Decker, Pat Hughes, Phil Kavanaugh, Andrea Lyons, Sean MacCarthy, Terry MacCarthy, Dick Parsons, Eugene Pincham, Song Richardson, Jack Rimland, Steve Shanin, John Stobbs, Randy Stone, Judge Richard Walsh
Indiana:	Jodie English, Rick Kamman, Jim Voyles

Kansas: Professor Jim Jeans, Judge Joe Johnson, Judge Thomas Marten

Louisiana: Jim Boren, Mike Fontham, Bob Glass, Rebecca Hudsmith, Virginia Schlueter

Maine: Steve Schwartz

Maryland: Paul DeWolfe, Maureen Essex, Carmen Hernandez, Paul Mark Sandler

Massachusetts: John Curtin, Kevin Curtin, Jim Doyle, Joe Oteri, Collette Tvedt

Michigan: Judge Paul Borman, Jim Feinberg, Randall Karfonta, Jim Robinson, Marty Robinson

Minnesota: Andrea George, John Tierney, Bill Ward

Mississippi: Phil Broadhead, Chris Klotz, Tom Fortner

Missouri: Cathy Kelly, Norm London, Burt Shostak, Grant Shostak

Montana: Craig Shannon

Nebraska: Don Fiedler

Nevada: Amy Coffee, Scott Coffee, Annabelle Hall, Mace Yampolsky

New Jersey: Tom Campion, Rick Coglin, Judge John Hughes, Bruce Goldstein, Jack McMahon, Herb Stern

New Mexico: Barbara Bergman, Charlie Daniels, Jim McElhaney, Randi McGinn

New York: Robert Fogelnest, David Lewis, James Mercante, Barry Scheck, Kim Taylor Thompson

North Carolina: Lewis Allen, Fred Lind, Steve Lindsay

Ohio: Ron Bailey, Tom Coffee, Mike Dane, Charles E. Evans, Jerry Gold, Gerry Messerman, Crystal Richie

Oklahoma: Garvin Isaacs

Oregon: Dennis Rawlinson, Laurie Shertz

Pennsylvania:	Jim Wade
Rhode Island:	Rich Corley
South Carolina:	Dale Cobb, Gaston Fairey, Ashley Pennington
Tennessee:	Beth Ford, Henry Martin, Gerald Milton, Steve Oberman, Bob Ritchie
Texas:	Mark Bennett, Charles Gorham, Racehorse Haynes, Robert Hirschhorn
Utah:	Larry Weiss, Mike Wims
Vermont:	Peter Langrock
Virginia:	Peter Kenny, Mary Lynn Tate, John Zwerling
Washington:	George Bianchi, Tom Hillier, Roger Peven, Jeff Robinson, Irwin Schwartz, Bob Taylor
West Virginia:	Jim Brown, Steve Farmer
Wisconsin:	Keith Belzer, Steve Glynn, Jim Shellow, Dean Strang, Deja Vishney
Wyoming:	Terry Mackey, Mike O'Donnell, Bob Rose, Jr., Gerry Spence
Puerto Rico:	Joe Laws

About the Author

Terence F. MacCarthy has been the executive director of the Federal Defender Program in the U.S. District Court for the Northern District of Illinois for more than 40 years. He was selected for the position in 1966 by the judges of the District Court and the deans of the six Chicago law schools. The office is frequently mentioned as being one of the best defender offices in the country. In addition to his administrative responsibilities, Mr. MacCarthy continues to personally try cases and to train and assist his staff of 20 attorneys.

Mr. MacCarthy received a B.A. in philosophy from St. Joseph's College in 1955 and a J.D. from DePaul Law School in 1960. He was a law clerk to former Chief Judge William J. Campbell of the U.S. District Court for the Northern District of Illinois and served as Illinois Special Assistant Attorney General, specializing in civil trials and appeals. His criminal experience is primarily in the federal courts, where he has tried and appealed many cases. He has argued before the U.S. Supreme Court. He is a sought-after speaker at continuing education programs, and has lectured in all 50 states and more than a dozen foreign countries.

Mr. MacCarthy has received numerous awards, including special awards from both his undergraduate college and his law school. He received the University of Virginia School of Law William J. Brennan, Jr. Award, the Harrison Tweed Special Merit Award from the ABA, and the Reginald Heber Smith Award from the National Legal Aid & Defender Association. In 2000 he received the "Defender of the Century" from the Federal Defenders Association and the Inns of Court Professionalism Award for the Seventh Circuit.

A member of the ABA for more than 30 years, Mr. MacCarthy has chaired the Criminal Justice Section and served on its council for more than 20 years, including seven as section representative in the House of Delegates. He served on the Board of Governors from 1997 to 2000.

1 Introduction

Most trial lawyers and an even greater number of trial advocacy teachers, and even some casual trial observers, are in general agreement that cross-examination is the skill most lacking in trial lawyers.

My own experiences buttress this conclusion. Having taught trial advocacy to thousands of lawyers, I am convinced that cross-examination is the most difficult skill for a trial lawyer to learn. Interestingly, I believe direct examination to be the second most difficult trial skill.

My epiphany came not in a courtroom but while teaching other lawyers. I have had the honor of teaching at the National Criminal Defense College since its inception. In the early years, I lectured on opening statements. Teaching opening statements to my small breakout group (always eight lawyers) was a professional joy. I used the National Institute for Trial Advocacy (N.I.T.A.) teaching method. After the lawyers delivered their openings, I would invite critiques from the others in the group. What did the lawyer do well, and why? What did the lawyer do badly, and why? I would then critique. As intended and desired, the opening statements got better as we moved along. The day was personally and professionally fulfilling.

The day spent with the cross-examination group was a disaster. With the critique method, the results were far from satisfactory. The lawyers did not, as they did with opening statements, get better as the day went on.

In truth, the orientation lectures on cross-examination were more "this is what I can do," than "this is what you should be doing." Still, this alone would not explain the failure to improve.

The main problem, I accepted, was me. I was not a good cross-examiner, and therefore I could not effectively teach cross-examination.

Frustrated, I finally asked the dean for a "float" on cross-examination day to visit many of the practice sections. I purposely visited those I thought would have the better teachers of cross-examination.

To my surprise and disappointment, what I saw was essentially what I had experienced. If the lawyers improved at all, it was not by much. There was a problem, but it was not me.

The following year I abandoned the N.I.T.A. system of post-critiquing. Rather, I immediately interrupted the lawyer when he or she did something wrong. The amazing result was that I better appreciated how one should cross-examine. Also, I was demonstrating and teaching the group, which, similar to the opening statement group, did improve as the day went on. This was a wonderful experience.

Over the next few years, the teaching opportunities and several federal trials resulted in the development of my "contrarian" views about cross-examination. The system, though still developing, was born.

The actors and actresses at the college were the first to notice how well my cross-examination group was doing. Soon other faculty, those with "floats," came by to see what we were doing.

Next, the dean asked me to put what I was doing into a talk. Since then I have switched from lecturing on opening statements to giving the orientation talk on cross-examination. I have given this cross-examination talk in all 50 states.

In addition to teaching lawyers, I have also had the honor to sit for many years as a judge-evaluator in the finals of the ABA Criminal Justice Section—John Marshall Law School trial advocacy competition. The young men and women who participate in this excellent program are exceptionally well prepared. Indeed, they should be. They will have tried the same case several times before they appear in the finals. Their trial advocacy teachers, who are more coaches than law professors, do a wonderful job of preparing their teams.

That said, year after year, these committed law students deliver outstanding closing arguments and excellent opening statements. Yet once a witness is put on the stand, the quality of trial advocacy diminishes. The direct examinations are not done particularly well, and the cross-examinations are the weakest aspect of the presentations.

This book is the long-overdue result of my learning experience. If trial lawyers are not particularly adept at cross-examining witnesses, we must reconsider what we have been taught about the purpose, methods, and execution of cross-examination in order to change our methods for the better. That, then, is the purpose of this book. I encourage you to consider a different cross so you can cross with a difference. We can no longer afford to retain a neophobic fear of change.

One reason lawyers cross-examine poorly is that they do not understand the purpose of cross-examination. It is hard to perform well when you do not understand what, let alone why, you are doing what you are doing. Too often, lawyers stand up thinking "This witness has hurt our case; therefore, I must hurt him." But with that method of cross-examination, we can only hurt each other. In other words, witness hurts us, we hurt witness. The best we have done is to neutralize this witness, and that is only if we have done an outstanding cross of the hurting kind. If we do not do an outstanding job, the witness is a net negative for us. We want to turn the witness into a net positive for our case.

What, then, is the goal of cross-examination? Part of the problem is that leading lawyers, teachers, and commentators have filled us with incomplete or inaccurate answers. Now get ready to think about it in a different way.

The goal of any cross-examination always depends on the case and the witness. If you answered with things like "control," "extract admissions," or "discredit by challenging the witness's recollection," goals often suggested by a well-meaning evidence teacher, you get one star. Each of these goals is worthy, depending on the case and the witness. Many of these goals will have application to some part of most cross-examinations. However, none is relevant to every part of every cross-examination. To fashion a system cf cross-examination that works well in all kinds of cross-examinations and in all parts of a cross-examination, we must broaden our thinking from the cross-examination itself to the trial as a whole.

Answer a broader question. What is the goal of the trial lawyer with respect to the jury in every aspect of the trial? From voir dire through opening, direct, and cross-examination to closing argument? PERSUASION. We are trying to persuade the jury in a jury trial, or judge in a bench trial, to accept our client's version of the facts as told by us, the lawyer. And because that is our goal with the jury in the trial as a whole, why would it not also be our primary goal in cross-examination (as well as in every other aspect of the trial)?

With this premise in mind, that our goal is to persuade, let us re-examine the many misconceptions about cross-examination drilled into our heads by well-meaning but misguided lawyers, teachers, and commentators.

The goals handed down from sermons on the mount by evidence professors are proper goals of some portions of some cross-examination. But we are looking for a system that fits our goal of persuasion in every portion of every cross-examination. What do everyday people like you and me associate with the goals the evidence professor provided? Do the word association yourself: *controlling*—ex-wife or ex-husband; *extract*—dentist; and *discredit by challenging*—insult. Ask yourself, do you want to be seen by the jury as controlling, extracting, and insulting? I hope not. As trial lawyers, we want to *look good* in front of the jury. Because to look good is more persuasive than to seem to be controlling, extracting, and insulting.

My experience demonstrated that lawyers are most adept at opening and closing arguments, and least adept at cross- and direct-examinations. Why? There are several answers to this question, including the fact that opening statements and closing arguments are done by the individual lawyer and do not require the cooperation of a witness, either friendly or hostile. If you gave that answer, it is important but not primary. This book will teach you how to look good and persuade even if the witness is not cooperating. The primary reason lawyers are more adept in opening statements and closing arguments is that they are able to use the most persuasive technique known—they are allowed to *tell a story*.

How, you must ask yourself, can one *look good telling a story* in cross-examination when you are required to ask questions and elicit answers from a hostile witness? Again, challenge your assumptions based on the teachings from the past. It would be easier if the witness did not have to participate, but nothing in the rules says you cannot minimize the witness's involvement without appearing controlling, extracting and insulting. Use *short statements* and make the witness affirm everything you say.

A summary of my preaching on cross-examination is best captured in these three themes, themes that will often reappear throughout this book. To improve and to change your thoughts on cross-examination, I suggest you seek, in cross-examination, to:

Look Good
Tell a Story
Use Short Statements

The Purpose of This Book

2

A. THE SYSTEM

There are three things I intend to do. First, and most important, I want to share with you a style and system of cross-examination. It will be a complete "turnkey" operation, one that will allow you to cross with systematic style. You can, and hopefully will, use it on every witness, and particularly on experts.

Candor requires me to confess that this style and system is contrary to the conventional wisdom, contrary to what you have been taught, and contrary to how most of you are now doing your cross-examinations.

The Litigation Section of the American Bar Association, a wonderful organization for which I have much respect and admiration, calls my style and system "contrarian." Interestingly, that same Litigation Section frequently invites me to share with them my "contrarian system." For that matter, I have, at the Section's request, produced tapes, in both video and audio, for the American Bar Association.

Contrarian though it is, this system has for many years also been taught at the National Criminal Defense College, as fine a trial advocacy program as has ever existed. For many years the system has also been taught at the outstanding Western Trial Advocacy Institute held in Wyoming every July. The system is also used by many outstanding trial lawyers, both criminal and civil. Recently

I was told it is being taught to assistant U.S. attorneys. In a word, it works extremely well.

B. CHANGE YOUR THINKING

My second purpose is to disabuse you of your concept, your macroscopic view of cross-examination: to destroy the witness.

You most probably came by your understanding of cross from criminal defense lawyers, who have been the teachers of cross, just as prosecutors have been the teachers of direct examination. Neither have done particularly well, which is a major reason why cross- and direct examination are the most difficult trial advocacy skills.

"Counsel, you may cross-examine" gets your adrenaline, if not your confidence, going. You think of Dean Wigmore's poignant reference to cross as "the greatest engine ever invented." You picture that engine as a large steel locomotive, one that pulls a train. In your mind's eye, you climb aboard, put on your engineer's cap, and throw additional coals on the fire. You are ready to take on the witness. Cross, you have been taught, is your opportunity to attack, pillage, and plunder. You will take no prisoners. You aim the locomotive engine at the witness and go right at him, knock him over and roll over him. Once past the witness, whom you have left on the ground, you do not continue forward. Rather, you slam on the brakes, put the locomotive in reverse, and back up over the witness so you can grind him or her into the ground.

Okay, this may be a slight overstatement of what you want to do—but not by much. Walk into any courtroom, watch Court TV, or reflect on your most recent cross. What you see, an astigmatism of advocacy, goes something like this:

> Q: (With a sneer and mean voice) Blah, blah, blah, blah, blah, blah, blah, blah (and probably even more blahs).

Translating the "blahs" might go something like this:

> Ma'am, isn't it true that on the night in question, there was a blinding snowstorm, it was pitch-black out, and when you exited your vehicle you were at a great distance from the liquor

store that you were going to in order to refill your brandy supply because you had run out during the day, and you had taken off your glasses at the time the robber ran quickly out of the store?

A: (also with a sneer, usually a lesser one, and corresponding mean voice) Blah, blah, blah, blah yourself.

Translation:

Actually, there was a light snow, and the parking lot was well lit. I parked in the handicapped spot and your client stopped to look at me as I got out of the car, and the brandy ran out a week ago when I had guests. I took my reading glasses off so I could get a better look at your client.

This back and forth dialogue almost always involves argument, bickering, and quibbling.

Q: You did not see the car, did you?
A: Yes, as I told you, I saw the car.
Q: From where you were standing you could not see the car, could you?
A: I am telling you, again, I saw the car.
Q: You could not see the car, isn't that correct?
A: How many times do I have to tell you I saw the car?

What we have here is "dialogue" cross-examination. First the lawyer speaks and then the witness speaks. Dialogue cross-examination results in arguing, bickering, and quibbling during cross. This means the lawyer is losing the battle. Cross-examination is not the time to engage in a "food fight," even if the witness is similarly obnoxious. With the awesome tools available to the cross-examiner, hectoring and pounding the witness into submission makes you look like a bully, particularly if the witness is less obnoxious than you are. As a good Irishman once said: "A true mark of character is how you handle power when you have it." Power wielded seamlessly and without being overbearing is the most effective and persuasive use of the power of cross-examination because you look good using it. Those who know how to use power effectively do not need to raise their voice, use a biting tone, or use any other disrespectful tactic. Letting the cross degenerate into arguing, bickering, and quibbling is disastrous.

Indeed, I have even seen dialogue cross-examinations where the witnesses will ask the cross-examining lawyer questions. Worse still, the lawyer will answer the questions from the witness. When this happens, you should switch positions with the witness. You are finished, and so is your client.

Recently we have read of famous or, if you prefer, infamous trials where much of the damaging evidence was elicited not during the direct, but during the cross-examination. This is a sin that cries to God for vengeance. Cross-examination is not the time for a dialogue. Rather, it is the time for a monologue. Or, as a bright young lawyer from Philadelphia told me some years ago, "Terry, I enjoy doing your soliloquy cross-examinations."

During cross-examination there can be only one speaker—you, the cross-examiner. Every story can have only one master, one narrator. So every cross-examination can have only one storyteller—you. The witness has, at best, a cameo role. The witness will appear in a "disjunctive" rather than "narrative" form (the importance of this will be explained later).

Some years ago, I was asked to speak to FBI special agents at one of their training programs. Specifically, I was asked to speak about both cross- and direct examination. I knew the two agents who asked me to participate relatively well, as I had cross-examined both on several occasions. After I agreed to speak, they related a conversation they had had while walking to my office. They told me that when I cross-examined them, they got the distinct impression that I neither needed nor wanted them in the courtroom. They added that they believed they could leave the witness stand and go get an early lunch, and that I would in no way miss them.

This was a great compliment and an excellent explanation of my cross-examination system.

I hope I have made the point that dialogue cross, and in particular "attack, pillage, and plunder" dialogue cross, is not favored. This conclusion is buttressed by John Mortimer's famed English barrister Horace Rumpole, who observed that cross-examination is ". . . not the art of examining crossly."

C. WHAT WILL WE SAY, TO WHOM, AND HOW?

Third and finally, assuming we (1) are willing to consider this new system and style of cross-examination, and (2) we accept that we will be doing monologue, and not dialogue, cross-examination, we realize that our cross-examination will be a story—indeed, a preliminary closing argument. This conclusion, though it sounds good, raises questions: If we are to be the only speaker, what are we going to say, to whom will we say it, and how will we say it?

1. What Are We Going to Say?

This is easy. Like all good trial lawyers, we are going to tell a story. Listeners usually enjoy stories, particularly if they are well told. In truth, every great trial lawyer I have seen or worked with—and there have been many—is a consummate storyteller.

The content for your story must come necessarily (and often unfortunately) from the facts of your case. Much has been said about the importance of having a theory of your case. Though obviously important, the fact is that your cases seldom present problems in ascertaining the theory. More important is listing the good *themes* available to you. Also, you must know (and factor into your consideration) the bad themes as well.

It is from these themes, both good and bad, that you prepare your story line. You intertwine them into the story you wish to tell. Good advocacy suggests that you present your themes with great gusto and, obviously, in the most favorable light possible.

To put you in the story mood, I have a suggestion, one I heard some years ago from a wonderful trial lawyer and great judge, William Bauer. He suggested that just before you start your story, you say to yourself, "Once upon a time . . . ." This will get you into storytelling mode and away from the all too common tendency of lawyers to give briefs rather than tell stories.

2. To Whom Are We Going to Tell Our Story?

This suggestion, in practice, will prove difficult for many, and others will question its wisdom. Simply stated, the story should be told to the people you want to hear it: the jury or, if a bench trial, the judge. To me, telling your wonderful story to "Perjuring Pete," the witness, makes

Exhibit 2-1
Federal Rule of Evidence 611

Rule 611. Mode and Order of Interrogation and Presentation

(b) Scope of cross-examination. Cross-examination should be limited to the subject matter of the direct examination and matters affecting the credibility of the witness. The court may, in the exercise of discretion, permit inquiry into additional matters as if on direct examination.

> "[T]rial judges retain wide latitude insofar as the Confrontation Clause is concerned to impose reasonable limits on such cross-examination based on concerns about, among other things, harassment, prejudice, confusion of the issues, the witness' safety, or interrogation that is repetitive or only marginally relevant." *Delaware v. Van Arsdall,* 475 U.S. 673, 679 (1986).

Prior to the 1974 amendment establishing the current scope of Rule 611(b), the Rule provided that a witness could be cross-examined "on any matter relevant to any issue in the case, including credibility." Fed. R. Evid. 611, advisory committee's note to subdivision (b) 1974 enactment. The current Rule provides that cross-examination should be lim-

little sense. And yet, probably because most cross-examination traditionally involves back-and-forth dialogue rather than storytelling monologue, most cross-examinations are between the lawyer and the witness. This is what we have learned and what we have been doing. This habit of talking to the witness will be most difficult to change.

When working with small groups, I have had success when I stand in front of the witness to block the witness from the cross-examiner. Considering my size, this is easily accomplished. I then remind the lawyer to look at and tell the story to the jurors. This is not a drill I use early in the day but later, when the lawyers have become familiar with the basic system. This method of teaching has still other benefits. The cross-examiner becomes less "cross" and improves on her storytelling.

A few years ago, a highly respected trial lawyer questioned the wisdom of not talking exclusively to the witness. This was how he had, with great success, conducted his cross-examinations. Considering the respect I had for this lawyer, I raised this issue—not with other ited to the subject matter of the direct examination and matters affecting credibility of the witnesses. Fed. R. Evid. 611(b). *See, e.g., United States v. Vasquez,* 858 F.2d 1387, 1392 (9th Cir. 1988) permitting cross-examination regarding narcotics and cash found in defendant's apartment as "reasonably related" to defendant's direct testimony when defendant testified on direct about the events leading up to his arrest, including the fact that he left his apartment alone at a certain hour on the day of his arrest.

Federal Rule of Evidence 611(b) also provides: "[t]he court may, in the exercise of discretion, permit inquiry into additional matters as if on direct examination." *See, e.g., United States v. Harbour,* 809 F.2d 384, 389 (7th Cir. 1987) (permitting cross-examination regarding defendant's selling of federal commodities when defendant chose to place the issue in dispute on direct with an outright denial of having ever sold commodities); *United States v. Moore,* 936 F.2d 1508, 1518-19 (7th Cir. 1991) (trial court properly denied cross-examination regarding the content of co-defendant's conversation with law enforcement upon arrest when the officer volunteered on direct the fact that he had a conversation with co-defendant about the crime after co-defendant's arrest, but made no mention of the content of the conversation).

lawyers (I assumed they would not favor talking to the jurors), but with two outstanding communicators who regularly teach trial advocacy. They had seen my method of cross-examination.

I was encouraged by the communicators' response. "Telling your story to the jury made sense," they told me. However, they did caution against being too obvious and too obsequious. From time to time you should, they suggested, look at the witness. Because my system does require occasionally looking at the witness, their suggestion was easy to accept.

For that matter, I recalled I had for some years suggested that when cross-examining a witness (assuming you are not using "one word" cross-examination), you should begin your statement looking at the witness and end looking at the jury. This directs the story to the jury. Conversely, on direct examination you would be advised to do exactly the opposite. On direct examination you want the story focused on your witness. Example on cross-examination:

Q. You saw (to witness) a green car? (to jury)

As is usually the case, you conduct direct examination in the exact opposite fashion. Example on direct examination:

Q. What color (to jury) was the car you saw? (to witness)

3. How Are We Going to Say What We Have to Say?

What is the best way to tell a story? How do you improve your communication skills? Let's face it, being a successful trial lawyer requires being a successful communicator. You are a salesperson—not much different from the person selling siding, used cars, or insurance policies.

Often lawyers tell me that being a trial lawyer requires, first and foremost, knowledge of the rules of evidence, which they urge are more important than communication skills. Actually, knowing both would be a great start. As to the relative importance of the two, I have been heard to say (irreverently) that "knowing evidence is not that important." I explain that "some judges do not know evidence, so why do you have to know evidence?"

Some years ago I had the pleasure of teaching a young lady who was a civil litigator in Ohio. When I work with good civil trial lawyers, I encourage them to visit their local courthouse and volunteer to take appointments to represent those who cannot afford counsel in criminal cases. This will, I explain, give them the trial experience they otherwise would not usually get as civil litigators. For an interesting comment about the difference between litigators and trial lawyers, see *In re Bristol-Myers Squibb Securities Litigation,* 228 F.R.D. 221, 230 (D.N.J. 2005). Magistrate Judge John J. Hughes, an experienced and able trial lawyer, obviously concerned about the civil trial lawyers' apparent unwillingness to try the case, said:

> Finally, claims of Plaintiff that it was necessary to await decision on various dispositive motions or other developments in the case before seeking to add new alleged misrepresentations are illusory. The new claims could have been added after depositions of the speakers had been conducted or cer-

> tainly before eight months had passed after the conclusion of fact discovery. There will always be more to "discover" and more to do in a case of this magnitude. The real issue is whether the Plaintiff class has had a full and fair opportunity to conduct discovery and adequately plead its case. The answer is a resounding yes. Illustrative is the comment widely attributed to Terence F. MacCarthy, Esquire, Federal Defender in Chicago: *The difference between trial lawyers and litigators is that litigators are always prepared but never ready.* This case is now ready for final resolution. An appropriate Order accompanies this Memorandum.

A few years after our first meeting, the young lady and I ran into each other at another trial advocacy seminar. She, with much pride and excitement, shared with me this story.

She followed through on my suggestion, though she did not go to her local courthouse; rather, she went to the federal court. She was appointed to represent one of several defendants in a bank robbery case that went to trial. Her defendant was acquitted. This is an unusual occurrence in federal court, particularly in bank robbery cases. After the trial, the trial judge called her into chambers. He told her she knew less evidence than any trial lawyer who had ever tried a case before him. However, he said, she was a wonderful communicator, and that is why she won the case.

One could and probably should write a book on communications for trial lawyers. In more recent years, seminars have wisely started to include communication as part of their curriculum. Josh Karton, a Californian, is far and away the best trial communications teacher with whom I have worked.

In any event, because this is not a book on communications as such, we will merely brush the surface.

Eye Contact

The most important requirement for good communications is to look at those with whom you are communicating. Eye contact is essential. This is not to suggest you stare at one of the jurors; that would make the juror feel uncomfortable. Rather, you should briefly look at all of the jurors in no particular order or sequence. The importance of looking at those to whom you are talking cannot be overemphasized.

The importance of eye contact came up in a legal though non-trial advocacy context in *United States v. Zambrana,* 428 F.3d 670 (7th Cir. 2005). The Seventh Circuit, in effect, agreed with a law enforcement officer that the driver of a car who did not make eye contact with the officer was acting sufficiently unusual to justify a stop. From this we can surmise that you should make eye contact with a police officer or risk looking unusual.

3 A Brief Interlude

For years I would start my cross talks with a story—more appropriately, a joke. As the years passed, I decided I had too much substance to cover and the story/joke went by the wayside. This book format allows me to share my story, which involves cross-examination. I cannot and do not claim the story is true. It may be, but I leave that decision to you.

Chicago is in Cook County, Illinois. Cook County has the largest court system in the world. For historical reasons that are better not revealed, a large majority of Cook County's criminal cases, particularly the more significant cases, are processed and tried at a major courthouse at 26th and California. The courthouse is 26 blocks south of Madison Street and 28 blocks west of State Street. It is not in the Loop or downtown.

A large majority of the state's attorney's staff and the public defender staff are housed at 26th and California. The venue of this story is there.

A young public defender was appointed to represent a defendant who was charged with murder and, obviously, in jail. The young defender visited with his new client in the lockup. He obtained what information he could from the defendant. He then thoroughly investigated the case.

Upon completing his investigation, the public defender returned to the lockup. With much trepidation, he explained to the defendant that the case against him was very solid. He could find no theory to defend the case. He strongly suggested the defendant plead guilty and throw himself on the mercy of the court.

The defendant was understandably disappointed with this report and adamantly said he would not plead guilty. He reminded the young public defender that he, the public defender, was in the public defender's office to get trial experience and indeed he could win this case; that it was he, the defendant, who would make the decision whether to plead or go to trial; and finally having made that decision, he opted for a jury trial.

Young, and surely old, public defenders know the drill: The theory of the case would be "play for the fumbles."

The defendant did get a slight break. Doctor Smith, who performed the post mortem on the body of the dead man and wrote the autopsy report, passed away three days before the trial was set to start. The young prosecutor anticipated a problem: How would he prove the *corpus delicti* without Dr. Smith?

Fortunately, prosecutorial offices, and defender offices as well, have experienced lawyers. Among other things, they are there to help and advise the younger, less-experienced lawyers. So it was that the young prosecutor presented his dilemma to an older prosecutor. The answer was simple, explained the older prosecutor. They should get another doctor. He suggested Doctor Young, who was new to the area. Doctor Young would be asked to read Doctor Smith's report, and based upon that, he could and would satisfy the *corpus delicti* requirement. Though not totally convinced, this made some sense to the young prosecutor.

The trial began. Within five minutes of the prosecutor's opening statement, the jury was ready to convict. Unfortunately, as often happens, the young prosecutor continued to "bore" on. Six minutes after the start of the prosecutor's opening statement, many of the jurors were asleep and all had stopped listening. This was not necessarily good for the defendant, however, as the jurors had tuned out with visions of conviction in their heads.

The public defender's opening statement was a cross between the two defense opening statements in the movie *My Cousin Vinny*. It did nothing to wake the sleepers nor interest those who were semi-awake. Juror apathy and disinterest continued throughout the trial. This was, the jurors correctly believed, nothing like the interesting trials they saw on television and at the movies. This lack of involvement continued until the cross-examination of the prosecutor's last witness, Dr. Young.

On direct examination, Dr. Young continued the boring theme by testifying he had read Dr. Smith's report, explained its conclusions, and thus satisfied the abstract *corpus delicti* requirement.

Up till then, the public defender had done nothing—indeed, he had no tools with which to do anything. Though boring, the young prosecutor had not fumbled. Now the cross.

Defender: It would be fair to say that everything you know about this case and everything you have told us you learned from reading Dr. Smith's report?

Doctor Young: Yes, that is right.

Defender: So if Dr. Smith made a mistake in preparing his report, you would have repeated that mistake?

Doctor Young: Well, yes.

Defender: If Dr. Smith left something out of his report, that would have been a mistake?

Doctor Young: Yes.

Defender: If Doctor Smith put something in his report that did not belong in the report, that would have been a mistake?

Doctor Young: Yes.

Defender: Of course, you cannot tell us that Dr. Smith did not leave something out of his report?

Doctor Young: No, I cannot.

[For the first time since the early minutes of the prosecutor's opening statement, the jurors were now awake. This was interesting and appeared important. This was more like the television and movie trials.]

Defender: You cannot tell us that Dr. Smith did not put something in the report that did not belong.

Doctor Young: No.

Defender: You were not present when Dr. Smith did his autopsy?
Doctor Young: No.
Defender: You did not talk to Dr. Smith before he prepared his report?
Doctor Young: No.
Defender: You did not talk to Dr. Smith after he prepared his report?
Doctor Young: No.
Defender: So you actually never talked to Dr. Smith about this report?
Doctor Young: That's right.
Defender: As a matter of fact, you never talked to Dr. Smith about any of his reports?
Doctor Young: No.
Defender: You never even met Dr. Smith?
Doctor Young: No. I heard he was a fine man but I never met him.

[The public defender, emboldened by his minor success, goes to a new point.]

Defender: You never saw John Jones (the dead fellow) when he was supposedly alive?
Doctor Young: No.
Defender: You never saw the supposed body of the supposed John Jones when he was supposedly dead?
Doctor Young: No.
Defender: As a matter of fact you cannot be sure John Jones is really dead?

[The public defender was letting it all hang out—this was his one chance. The now much awake and receptive jurors were on the edge of their chairs. This was the case.]

Doctor Young: No, counsel, I cannot be sure John Jones is really dead. But I can be sure of two things. First, I can be sure that back in my laboratory on the third shelf from the top I have the brain of John Jones. Secondly, I can be sure if he is alive he is practicing as a criminal defense lawyer someplace.

4 An Early Cross-Examination: Susanna and the Elders

Going back to the Old Testament, the 13th chapter of the *Book of Daniel*, we see the necessity and the power of cross-examination.

Susanna was a very beautiful woman who was married to Joachim, a wealthy man. Joachim had an orchard near his house. As was her custom, Susanna, after guests left around noon, would repair to the orchard, where she would bathe and wash herself.

Two older men, elders, who were frequent guests at Joachim's house, "were inflamed with lust towards" Susanna. They hid and watched every day to see her going to the orchard. She went with two maids who brought her oil and washing balls, and then the maids shut the door and left her alone to wash herself.

One day when the maids had gone, the two elders came out of hiding and ran to Susanna. They told her the doors were shut so no one could see them and declared they were in love with her. She, they explained, had a choice: Either she could lie with them or, if she refused, they would "bear witness . . . that a young man was with thee." This was the reason, they would say, why she sent her maids away. Susanna realized that if they told this untruthful story, it would probably be believed and she would be put to death.

Being a woman of virtue, Susanna refused to lie with them, and they followed through with their threat. They testified that a young man lay with her, which they said they saw from a corner of the orchard. They testified they ran up to the couple and tried to catch the young man, but he was too strong for them and escaped from the orchard by leaping over a wall. They further testified that she refused to tell them who the young man was.

The perjurers were believed, and Susanna was condemned to death. Susanna cried out (appealed!), seeking God's help. And help He did. In what may have been the first appointment of counsel, God appointed a young boy named Daniel to represent Susanna.

Daniel, no doubt, was an early public defender. He reminded the people they had convicted her "without examination or knowledge of the truth." Daniel then asked that the two elders be separated, or sequestered, as we would say, and cross-examined each of them.

His cross-examination primacy was, to say the least, a bit excessive—indeed, totally abusive. No wonder we like to cross-examine that way! But then he got to his story line. He asked the first elder "under what tree the two had been." "The mastic tree" was the answer. Daniel then asked the second elder the same question. This time the response was "under the holm tree." Susanna's life was saved, thanks to this effective cross-examination by the young appointed lawyer, Daniel.

As we will soon see, we are most pleased with the result, though we are not pleased with the form used.

5

The Bad, the Ugly, and the Good

Before presenting the system, I offer a few comments about cross-examination as it exists today. First I have some bad news for you. I also have some ugly news. Finally, I have some good news.

A. THE BAD NEWS

There are five things that attorneys may want to and be allowed to do in a trial: voir dire, opening statements, cross-examination, direct examination, and closing arguments. Of all those things we do in a trial, the most difficult thing is to cross-examine,[1] for three reasons.[2]

1. The Witness

The first and most obvious reason why cross is difficult is because of the witness. That witness has been put on the stand by your opponent. He or she is not there to help you, but to hurt you. As a criminal defense attorney, that witness is there to put your client in jail. In the civil area,

1. Understand that I did not say cross-examination was the most important thing. Voir dire and, in particular, the opening statements are usually more important. Then again, everything we do during trial is important.

2. If you learn nothing else from this book, you are going to learn about the persuasive power of trilogies. Anytime there are reasons for something, there will be three reasons. If you only have two, make up a third. If you have four, eliminate one.

that witness is there to keep money from you or to give money to the other side.

2. The *Perry Mason* Syndrome

The second reason cross-examination is difficult is the *Perry Mason* syndrome. Most of us have seen *Perry Mason* on television. In particular, we have learned about cross-examination from *Perry Mason.* Perry Mason won every case he ever tried, and he won them all through cross-examination. No one has ever seen Perry Mason deliver a closing argument; he has never had to give one.

You know the scene. The witness is on the stand, and Perry stands up to cross-examine him. After a few minutes of Perry's (truth be known) not particularly good cross-examination, the witness starts to fall apart. Finally, he breaks down, shakes his head and says, "No, Mr. Mason, I've got to tell you the truth. It wasn't your Johnny that robbed the bank, it was me." Everybody in the courtroom shouts "hallelujah!," the judge dismisses the case, and the prosecutor, Hamilton Berger, goes back and gets reelected. That is what always happens.[3]

As a long-time criminal defense lawyer who has lost many cases, I was surprised to note that the *Perry Mason* trials always have music. I would welcome music, particularly if I could, as Perry does, orchestrate it. I have never tried a case with musical background.

Maybe Perry's success suggests that we as trial lawyers should simply rent all of the Mason shows. Could we watch them and learn? Hardly. Perry is a terrible cross-examiner but a wonderful actor. Then why does he always win? He wins for three reasons: He has (1) a great investigator, (2) a wonderful and devoted secretary, and, most important, (3) because he writes the script. Why does he always win during cross-examination? Cross-examination is the sexiest part of the trial, particularly a criminal trial.

The problem with the highly entertaining *Perry Mason* shows is that everybody's exposed to them. There is a good chance that some, if not all, of your jurors have seen Perry. You certainly have. An expectation factor has been created, both in the jury and, more destructively, in you as the cross-examiner.

---

3. Incidentally, how can you explain Hamilton Berger constantly being reelected as the district attorney? He seldom, if ever, won a case. Certainly he never won against Perry Mason.

Whenever a lawyer gets up to cross-examine, particularly in criminal cases, the jury expects you to do something really dynamic and case-decisive. Juror expectation is a minor problem compared to the *Perry Mason* syndrome's effect on lawyers. Lawyers, particularly criminal defense lawyers because we do so much cross-examination, are also subject to the *Perry Mason* syndrome. We expect that we will get witnesses to fall apart, to literally confess that they are liars and usually felons, the way witnesses always did for Perry Mason.

Imagine you have a witness on the stand. Imagine the witness was mugged at 11:00 p.m., under a viaduct,[4] as she was walking home from a bar. Now she is in court on direct and she testifies that it was your client who mugged her. You have to cross-examine her.

At this point, the *Perry Mason* syndrome makes lawyers think that they can get her to change her mind to the point that she will break down and say, "Oh, counsel, I can't live this lie any longer. It wasn't your Johnny who mugged me. It was—it was the prosecutor over there who mugged me!" This does not happen.[5] Nevertheless, the *Perry Mason* syndrome has programmed us to hold these dramatic images as the ideal to be strived for. This programming causes problems. We think we can get this witness to switch stories. By harboring unrealistic expectations, we hamper our efforts to reach realistic and attainable goals.

An excellent New York trial lawyer, having heard my talk on cross-examination, commented and complimented me on making this point.

---

4. "Viaduct" is a term used by Midwesterners to refer to what the remaining English-speaking world calls an overpass.

5. Despite our expectations, few lawyers are prepared for the consequences of an actual *Perry Mason* experience. In truth, they have no reason to be. In more than 40 years of running a federal defender office, we have had one *Perry Mason* trial, and that was some 25 years ago. One of the lawyers in my office was doing a cross in a gun possession case. During the case, the witness suddenly said, "I can't go on with this. Those weren't Johnny's guns, those were my guns." Mind you, this was not in response to anything earth-shattering that the cross-examining attorney had done. Being an experienced veteran, the lawyer doing the cross did what any of us would have done: He froze. He looked at the witness. He looked at the judge. The judge was not sure what to do. After several minutes of silence, with everybody looking at each other, the prosecutor finally said, "Well, Your Honor, may we move on?" To which the judge replied, "No, I don't think we are going to move on." It took a recess to figure out what to do. Eventually, the case was dismissed. This was the only *Perry Mason* experience enjoyed by our office.

As he puts it, a cross-examiner seldom wins with a knockout, but rather should strive to win on points with jabs, counterpunching, and defensive boxing.

3. Old School Cross-Examination

The third and, indeed, the major problem with cross-examination is the long-accepted conventional wisdom on how to do cross-examinations: how you have been taught. Most of you were first taught in law school. That is an interesting experience. In some law schools, trial advocacy is taught by people who have tried few cases. In other law schools, trial advocacy professors are experienced and excellent.

You also may have learned to cross-examine by attending seminars. Who is the speaker on cross-examination? It is always some well-known lawyer who just won (or lost, if they do criminal defense) some major case.[6] They are always marvelous lawyers, but their talks on cross-examination are, by and large, anecdotal. They tell you about some of their great cross-examinations, and often they read to you from their transcripts.

I will tell you two things about lecturers reading from transcripts. First, any time you see a lawyer read from a transcript, the transcript has been edited. Anyone who has done any appellate work knows that there has never been an intelligible unedited transcript that can be read from. Second, whenever you see a criminal defense lawyer read from a transcript, you know he or she lost the case. We, as criminal defense lawyers, do not get transcripts unless we lose the case.

The problem with the typical talk on cross-examination is that it tells you more about what a good cross-examiner the speaker is than how to be a good cross-examiner yourself. After hearing about or reading someone else's brilliant cross-examination, the people who heard the talk or read the transcript can now do a better job on cross, as long as their next case has facts identical to those heard or read. Somehow, when you try to do what that great cross-examiner did,

6. By the way, it is always somebody from out of town. This is because most lecturers on cross-examination are criminal defense lawyers. For every spectacular case won by any criminal defense lawyer who tries cases on a regular basis, that same lawyer has 10 clients in jail. For this reason, lecturers on cross-examination are never local; advice is taken far more easily from someone whom you have not heard of or seen lose cases in the past.

your witness does not respond the same way. No single organized system has been presented for you to follow. And so attorneys do not improve as they would like to.

Why is there no chorus of complaints about this failure within our profession? Why do we accept a system that fails to teach us how to cross-examine effectively? There are, of course, three reasons. First of all, we accept it because we don't know any better. Second, we accept it because no one wants to stand up and complain about it; no one wants to declare that the emperor is naked. To do so would be to admit that our own cross-examination skills need help. And finally, we do not complain because we have been told that cross-examination is an art. We have been told that if we cannot cross-examine, this is understandable. We cannot cross-examine for the same reason that many of us cannot sing well. It is a talent that you must be born with or you will never have it.

There is a tremendous pedigree to this notion that cross-examination is an art. The Bible of cross-examination is a once-popular book, *The Art of Cross-Examination*, published by Collier Books and written by Francis L. Wellman, an outstanding turn-of-the-century trial lawyer who practiced in New York. When I graduated from law school and announced to the world my ambition to be a trial lawyer,[7] I was told that I had to read Wellman. Wellman wrote about the great and near-great lawyers of his time and those before his time. When I first read it, *The Art of Cross-Examination* was wonderful reading.

More than 20 years ago when I was working on this system, I reread Wellman. It remained interesting, but now I realized it was not a tool for teaching cross-examination. Apart from the interesting historical stories of history, Wellman's most significant contribution was his belief that cross should be conducted differently from direct. Go into courtrooms throughout our country and it becomes obvious that this distinction is not always observed.

This idea that cross-examination is an art was further perpetuated in the New Testament of cross-examination: the articles and, in par-

7. In those days, declaring that one was going to be a criminal defense lawyer was greeted with the same enthusiasm that would be expected after declaring that one was going to sell heroin. In this context, I am reminded of the popular T-shirt frequently found at criminal defense lawyer and defender seminars or conferences: "Please don't tell my mother I'm a public defender, she thinks I work in a whorehouse."

ticular, the riveting talk of Professor Irving Younger. Irv Younger was, in my opinion, the greatest speaker in the history of continuing legal education. Younger, as did Wellman before him, told us that cross-examination is an art. He said that you must have tried at least 25 cases before you can even consider yourself ready to learn how to cross-examine. He also said there are less than 10 good cross-examiners in the United States. If we were to accept these statistics, it is no wonder most cross-examinations are not particularly good. Have we given up the effort to become good cross-examiners because Wellman and Younger have told us it is relatively impossible?

Although both Wellman and Younger, because of their deserved status and ability, still have some validity, I have come to doubt both the Bible and New Testament of cross-examination. Some years ago I had to put together a talk on impeaching witnesses. I reread Wellman's chapter on impeachment and realized that it was completely useless as a teaching aid. In the entire chapter, there was not one good cross-examination. It was and is great history, but you cannot learn to cross-examine from Wellman.

What about the New Testament of cross-examination? Irv Younger gave us the Ten Commandments of Cross, which many of us much appreciated but struggled to follow for years. The problem with Younger is that he was primarily an evidence teacher, not a trial lawyer. Younger was a phenomenal evidence teacher. He made the subject come alive. But if you pay close attention to the cross-examination portions of his talk, you will realize that they do not always make sense. Trial lawyers have known this for years, but few wanted to say too much.[8]

Cross-examination is difficult to begin with, and, by and large, we have not been taught to cross-examine effectively. Moreover, we have, in effect, been told that we should not expect to be taught to cross-examine effectively; as an art form, it is something that can only be learned through years of experience, combined within innate talents that few people are born with.

---

8. *See* Henry W. Asbill, The Ten Commandments of Cross-Examination Revisited (Section of Criminal Justice, American Bar Association, Winter 1994).

B. THE UGLY NEWS

The bad news produces the ugly news. Because of the way that trial advocacy is taught, because of anecdotal lectures that have no point to them, and because we have been told that cross-examination is an art, most cross-examinations in the United States are broken down into three parts. Walk into any courtroom in the United States today and this is essentially what you will see.

The Salutation

Let us assume again that the witness has been mugged and has said on direct that my Johnny was the mugger. During the first part of most cross-examination, the cross-examiner is as nice as can be. We invoke whatever ritual incantations we have been taught.[9]

> *Attorney:* Good morning, Ms. Jones. I hope you had a good trip to the courtroom this morning. You did not get rained on, I hope. Now, can you hear everything I say? If you cannot hear everything I say, you let me know; I will speak louder. I only have a few questions for you. This won't take much time. Can we agree that all of the questions I'm going to ask you can be answered with a "yes" or a "no?"

And then we love to start: "Now, on direct examination you testified that . . . ." For some reason we love that stupid phrase. If you ever use that phrase again, you should have your tongue cut out. For one thing, if the witness said something on direct, in all probability it is something your opponent wanted the witness to say. Why repeat it to the jury? Furthermore, the other side's witnesses do not "testify." The other side's witnesses "claim," or they "give their versions." Better yet, they "tell their stories," but they never "testify." The only witnesses who "testify" are your witnesses. Why? Because "testify" carries the image of a fiery tongue coming down from heaven revealing the truth. But still we start our cross-examinations with "on direct, you testified . . . ." That is the way our trial advocacy instructor started his or her cross-examinations, so that is how we do it as well.

9. In the words of the old trial lawyers with whom I worked, "You slather them up and down."

We have been talking, of course, of the salutation phase of cross-examination. We like to go through all kinds of rituals to get us started. We are simply repeating nineteenth-century trial advocacy techniques. Jurors dislike these salutations because they are dumb and boring.[10]

If the way we begin our cross-examinations were not bad enough, our stupid salutations have denied us the use of primacy. What people hear first they remember best. This will be covered later. This useless salutation, the primary or first stage of cross-examination, makes up about 10 percent of the entire cross.

The Begging

The second stage of cross-examination is the "begging" stage. This takes roughly 20 percent of the total cross-examination. The begging stage of cross-examination might go something like this:

Q: So you're not sure who it was who mugged you, are you?
A: Yes, I'm sure who it was.
Q: OK, maybe you are, but you can't be absolutely sure it was Johnny, my client.
A: Yes, I can be. It was Johnny, your client.
Q: But you're not absolutely, 100 percent positively, beyond all reasonable doubts sure it was Johnny, are you?
A: Yes, I am. I never forget a face, and I'll certainly never forget his face.

The more you beg, the more powerful the witness gets and the closer Johnny gets to jail. The begging stage is seldom, if ever, successful. If it is even slightly successful, we sit down. By sitting down, we do Johnny a big favor. We slow down the process of putting him in jail.

---

10. The Duke University anthropology school did a linguistic study on what jurors like and dislike in witnesses and lawyers. William M. O'Barr, Linguistic Evidence: Language, Power, and Strategy in the Courtroom (1982). Some of the ideas that I present have been extrapolated from that study. In that study, they learned that jurors hate when lawyers go through all that "would you like some coffee and donuts before you start" nonsense. Interestingly, I have recently seen judges stating trial rules that forbid the use of these salutations. I doubt the purpose is to make us better trial lawyers, but rather to protect the judge from abject boredom.

The Attack

However, if begging fails us, as it usually does, we enter the third and final phase of cross-examination. This is 70 percent of almost every cross-examination you see. This is the stage where you finally come to the realization that this lousy witness is there to hurt you and Johnny. You do not mind her hurting Johnny, but your reputation as a trial lawyer is important. Johnny will get over the jail thing eventually. But you, on the other hand, do not like to lose a trial.

So you say to yourself, "I'm smarter than this witness. Not only that, but I have at my disposal what Dean Wigmore called the 'greatest legal engine ever invented for the discovery of the truth.'" You picture or think of cross-examination as a gigantic locomotive, with you as the engineer. With your engineer's cap on, you climb up into the driver's seat. At this point, you are done with the incantations and through with the begging; you have now entered the attack, pillage, and plunder phase of cross-examination. You will take no prisoners. The cross might go something like this:

Q: Mrs. Wiggins, you're 63 years old, isn't that correct?
A: Yes.
Q: That's pretty old, isn't it?
A: Well, I don't know. I . . . .
Q: Are you trying to tell us you are not old?
A: Well, I guess I am older than most.
Q: You don't see as well as you used to, do you?
A: No, not as good as I used to.
Q: That's for sure. In fact, you have to wear glasses, don't you?
A: Yes, as a matter of fact I do.
Q: But you weren't wearing your glasses that night, were you?
A: No, I wasn't.
Q: So you're old, you can't see very well, and you need your glasses. Without those glasses you can't see a damn thing, and you didn't have your glasses with you that night, isn't that correct?

And that is the cross-examination. When you finally sit down, Johnny is waiting for you. He greets you with a smile and tells you, "Great job, counsel. You ripped the hell out of her." This stage of cross-examination is very popular with clients and their relatives. Unfortunately, while your client is congratulating you, the jury is muttering to themselves: "That guy [meaning you] is an ass." Believe me, it is a mistake to let the client, a soon to be convicted felon, evaluate your cross.

These, then, are the problems we have with cross-examination.

For good reason, I tell very few war stories. Most of my war stories are in jail and would prefer not to be spoken of. But I will tell you one that makes this point more vividly than anything I could write.

Some years ago I was defending a bank robbery case. My Johnny walked into a bank armed with a radio, which he pointed at the teller. He turned it on and handed the teller a note demanding money. Of course, the note was on the back of his electrical bill, complete with his name and address. The teller gave him the amount of money he asked for.[11] Of necessity, the defense was the normal bank robbery defense: insanity. It is and always has been a lousy defense, but when it is the only thing you have, you live with it.

The prosecution put on its psychiatrist to claim that my client was sane. The psychiatrist, somewhat elderly, was not a particularly good psychiatrist or witness. Besides, my client was listening to radio stations we do not hear. When I cross-examined the psychiatrist, I ripped him apart. (This was before I started using the system.) This was not difficult to do. My cross was a hatchet job; I took out a hatchet and went after the witness. I started swinging and took off the left side of his head and then his right arm at the elbow. By the time I was finished, body parts were all over the courtroom.

The case went to the jury, and while they were deliberating, the young but able prosecutor, the experienced judge and I went to dinner. This was civility at its best. We had an interesting dinner. The conversation amounted to: "So why did you do that?," "That was really brilliant the way you did that," and "Don't you know anything

11. This was a case before the Federal Sentencing Guidelines went into effect, but it is interesting to note the effect of the Guidelines on sentencing in bank robbery cases. Judges no longer control sentencing. In bank robbery cases, the bank tellers do the sentencing. When someone robs a bank, the teller looks at the robber and decides if he or she likes the looks of the robber. Then they consult the chart in the Sentencing Guidelines that lists the amount taken and the corresponding sentence. If the teller likes the robber, he or she gives them no more than $4,998. If not, the teller gives him $50,000, regardless of what he asked for. That ensures that the bank robber will go to jail for a very long time.

about evidence?" All in all, the conversation was extremely helpful to each of us.

During this conversation, the judge looked at me and said: "Terry, by the way, you know more about psychiatry than anyone I have seen in a courtroom." Being my modest self, I acknowledged that, yes, I had really devastated the good doctor. The judge replied, "That is not what I was talking about." Defending myself, I suggested that my knowledge of psychiatry came across in the cross of the doctor. "Let's talk about your cross of the doctor," said the judge. "During that cross, did you ever bother to look at your jury?" My answer was, "Of course not. If I looked at the jury, I would be scared that I might take off a couple of my own toes with that hatchet I was swinging."

He said, "You should have looked at your jury, Terry. During the first third of the cross-examination, they were really with and for you. They didn't like the witness; he was obviously deceitful, and he did not know what he was talking about. But he was an older guy, and during the last two-thirds of your cross, every time you hit him, they bled with him. They felt sorry for this man, and you really overdid it. At the end of your cross, it was you they disliked." Of course, I immediately dismissed and discounted these comments.

Late the next day, the jury came back. Justice was done. We immediately filed the appeal, and, believe it or not, the Seventh Circuit reversed the conviction. The grounds for reversal are unimportant for our purposes; suffice it to say that they had nothing to do with cross-examination or, surprisingly enough, with incompetency of counsel.

The case was assigned to a new district court judge for retrial. It was strange trying the same case over again; with the transcript of the psychiatrist's earlier testimony, I was in the position civil lawyers with depositions luxuriate in all the time. Thinking of what the first judge told me, I used about half of the cross-examination that I had used the first time. Instead of a hatchet, I used a stiletto. Instead of shredding the psychiatrist to ribbons, I just took a bit off of his ear. My client walked away. For once, I had learned something without one of my clients having to pay for it. I learned from a wonderful federal judge.

That is the ugly news. Cross-examination is supposed to be an art, and if that is true, then the state of the art is lousy. As if that were not bad enough, we have been told that cross-examination is an art requiring the kind of talent that you are either born with or you will never have. If that were true, a few of you were born to be good at cross-examination, but the rest of you should go back to writing codicils for wills to protect homeless cats. That is what the conventional wisdom tells us.

C. THE GOOD NEWS

Here is the good news. Cross-examination is not an art, it is a science. As a science, it can be taught. More important, it can be learned. By anyone. That is what this book undertakes to do—to teach you a complete system of cross-examination, and how to do it in a courtroom. With a little patience and effort, you too can become an effective cross-examiner.

What about the idea that you have to be "born with it?" What about all those stories of lawyers who do the things that we would never think of or dare to do and get away with them? How can learning a system make us like them? Is not what they do an art? Maybe it is. Admittedly, there are a few lawyers who elevate cross-examination from a science to an art. But those are the rare exceptions.

Recall Babe Ruth. When Babe Ruth was in his heyday, he made hitting an art. He did not have to abide by all the rules. On the day of a ball game, Babe Ruth would go to the stadium and put on his pinstripes like everybody else. And when he finished putting on his uniform, you would think he would go out with the rest of the Yankees to do stretching exercises, run around the field a few times, and take batting practice. Not Babe Ruth. While the rest of Yankees were out there getting ready for the game, Babe Ruth went up in the stands, where they sold hot dogs and beer. He would order a dozen hot dogs and a few beers, then he would call over some young kids. He treated them, along with himself, to the hot dogs. The beers he kept for himself. That was his pre-game preparation. Belching and all, he hit home runs like no one before him and few since.

That was Babe Ruth. He could break all the rules and still be one of the greatest players who ever lived. There are lawyers like that, who elevate cross-examination to an art. They can and often do violate the rules. This does not mean you should violate the rules, unless you are, like them, a genius.

Parenthetically, this is one of our problems—when trial lawyers try, in their cross-examinations, to emulate genius lawyers. Not being born with these extraordinary talents, they are doomed to failure. There have been thousands of very good baseball players, and there have been less than a handful of Babe Ruths among them. That does not mean the rest are bad; it just means that they have to follow the rules.

Similarly, you can be a good cross-examiner without being one of the gifted few. You can learn. And that is what this book sets out to do.

6 Three Miscellaneous Considerations

A. THE PURPOSES OF CROSS-EXAMINATION: LOOKING GOOD

I am about to share with you a system and approach to cross-examination that is contrary both in practical application and in the underlying premises to much that you have learned about the subject. An example of this "contrarianism" arises immediately, as we discuss the purposes of cross-examination.

What are we seeking to do in cross-examination? According to the National Institute of Trial Advocacy, the three primary objectives of cross-examination are to obtain helpful information, to discredit witnesses or their testimony, and to bolster the credibility of persons who will subsequently discredit the witness and his or her testimony.[1] These are all worthwhile goals, but none are what I would consider to be the primary goals of cross-examination. The true objective of cross-examination, above all else, is to *look good*. You, the cross-examining attorney, want to look good. You want this jury to like you. The form of your cross-examination is more important than the substantive points you seek to make.

I realize that many—indeed, most of you—may be somewhat skeptical of this contention. Surely I am not

---

1. Scott Baldwin, *Cross-examination of Lay Witnesses,* in MASTER ADVOCATE'S HANDBOOK (D. Lake Rumsey ed., 1986).

saying that it makes no difference what questions I ask or what answers I receive. To some extent, however, that is exactly what I am saying. We live in an age of TV, of advertisements that do not show the product, of election of judges based on their surnames, and of the Home Shopping Network. Attention spans are at an all-time low. Ordinary people do not normally have to assimilate and process hours of oral information. And ordinary people do not change merely by becoming jurors; they continue to listen with their eyes and think with their emotions. "It is in the power over emotions that the life and soul of oratory is to be found." Aristotle, 350 B.C.

As an example of this, consider the following. I have lectured throughout the country on the topic of cross-examination, speaking at seminars and conventions. My audiences are usually trial lawyers, people who make their day-to-day living in courtrooms, trying cases. To these erudite audiences, I have raised the example of the trial scene from Scott Turow's excellent book and the wonderful movie, *Presumed Innocent*.

Admittedly, reference to the book and movie is far less effective today than when they first came out and were fresh in the audience's mind. A vast majority of my audiences have either read the book or seen the movie. A majority can still recall the trial scene, in which the prosecutor's pathologist is destroyed on cross-examination.

Many of you are familiar with *Presumed Innocent*. For those who are not, I would like to talk about the trial scene.

The prosecutors had put on a solid case to prove that the defendant was guilty of murder. Not unlike my little story in the introduction, they saved as their last witness the pathologist, Dr. Kumegai. His direct examination had apparently put the final nails in the defendant's coffin. There was no question that after Dr. Kumegai's direct, the jury would have convicted. In other words, the doctor "looked good" on direct. He spoke, usually to the jurors, as FBI special agents are taught to do: He "pointed with pride" and "viewed with alarm."

Then, of course, Sandy Stern, the defense attorney, stood up to cross-examine. Do you remember that? Stern called him "Painless" to start off. The witness did not like that. And then Stern went on to totally destroy the witness and, in so doing, destroyed the prosecution's case.

There is no question that, had the case gone to the jury, the verdict would have been a "not guilty," and it would have been a "not guilty" solely because of the cross-examination of Dr. Kumegai.

If you are familiar with *Presumed Innocent*, I have a question for you. You saw that movie or read that book through the eyes of a trial lawyer. Do you remember the substantive point made by Sandy Stern in that decisive cross-examination?

In my lectures across the country, I have asked this question of entire rooms full of trial lawyers. A majority of those lawyers had either seen the movie or read the book. And yet the number who actually could articulate the substantive point made in that cross-examination was less than one in 100. Think for a moment: If trial lawyers do not remember the substantive point, the jury probably never got it in the first place. What they saw, and remembered, was the form. During cross-examination the lawyer "looked good," the witness "looked bad."

After reading the book, I saw *Presumed Innocent* in the movie theater, and I myself still missed the substantive point. I knew that there was something about the victim using a diaphragm and having her tubes tied. I could see the inconsistency, but I failed to see how that made the defendant not the murderer. So after the movie I returned to the book and reread the cross-examination to see if I could find the substantive point made in the cross-examination. I did, finally. The next morning I called up the author, Scott Turow, who had been a most able assistant U.S. attorney, and asked him to explain it to me. He told me what he intended, and it made sense to me. The interesting thing is that, not only to the fictional jurors but to myself and everyone else who read the book or saw the movie, the prosecution's case was destroyed during that cross-examination without anyone understanding the substantive point. How did that happen? What *did* the jury get?

They saw the doctor, on direct examination, competently and calmly answering questions. On cross, they saw that same doctor flustered, at a loss for words, unable to explain himself. What it was that the doctor was unable to explain is irrelevant. To see what the jury saw, rent the movie and watch that trial scene with the sound off. You will see Sandy Stern handing Dr. Kumegai a document, and you will see Dr. Kumegai wilt. That is what the jury saw in that case, and that is what they are looking for in real life. They see form and not substance. It may be true that substance can be used to create form, but substance is not our ultimate goal. We are more interested in form than substance.

This is good news for all of us who try cases that are not sure-fire winners. This is especially good news for my public defender brothers and sisters, who most often have to try cases with no substance whatsoever on their side. Public defenders lose a lot of cases due to pesky substantive evidence. By concentrating on form, maybe they can actually win a case or two.

Scott Turow kindly gave me permission to reproduce the cross-examination of Dr. Kumegai. By rereading it, you can now observe that the substantive point was the strong suggestion that the doctor had the wrong autopsy report.

I have an analogy to help you understand what jurors see. Imagine an ordinary teeter-totter, of the sort found on playgrounds with liability insurance. Cross-examining attorneys and witnesses occupy opposite ends of that teeter-totter. If one end of a teeter-totter is up, the other end must be down. Every single witness, to different degrees, begins in an up position. The lawyer begins in the down position.

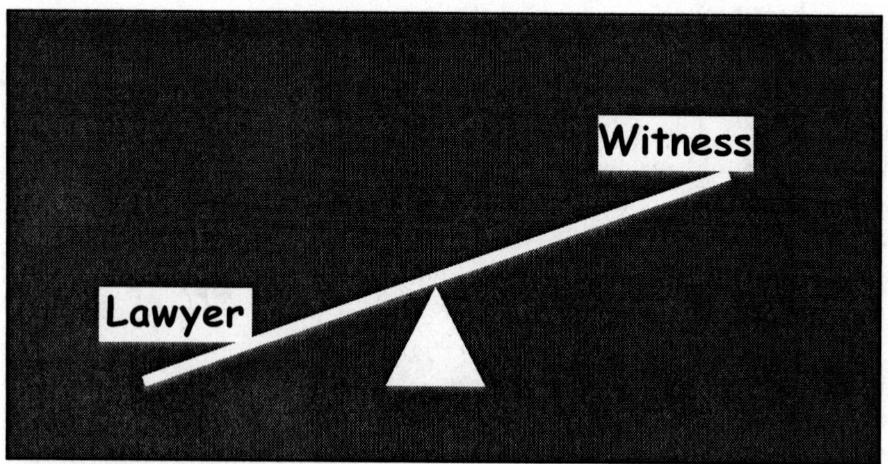

The object of cross-examination is to reverse that teeter-totter. How do you reverse the teeter-totter? Every time you look good, you go up one notch. And when you go up one notch, the witness automatically goes down one notch. Every time the witness does something to look bad, the witness goes down and you go up. Importantly, "looking bad" is more impactive than "looking good." The movement in terms of notches is multiplied. This observation suggests the obvious conclusion that we want to encourage the witness to "look bad." Thus, the object of cross-examination, as we are going to learn, is to end up something like this.

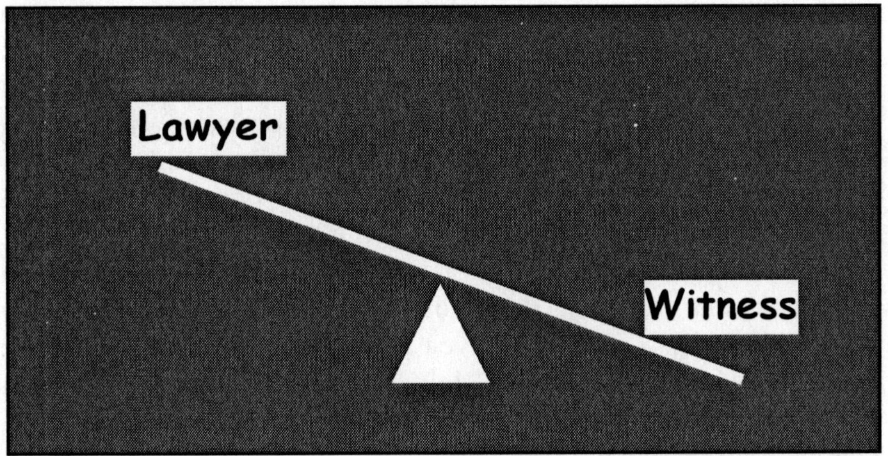

Now, certain witnesses start higher or lower than others. If, in an opening statement, you can tell the jury that the other side's witness has three convictions, that witness may be nearer the level of the lawyer to begin with. But in general, every witness is up and you, the big lawyer, are down. You have to change that. You change it by your "looking good," or getting the witness to "look bad." That will be our objective in cross-examination.

Do you remember the *Perry Mason* syndrome that was discussed in the introduction? We noted that one of the problems of modern cross-examinations is that lawyers are always looking to do what Perry Mason did—have the witness break down under cross-examination and admit that the defendant is not guilty. By keeping in mind that our purpose on cross-examination is merely to look good, we move away from these unrealistic expectations. Under the system of cross taught in this book, cross-examiners will not try to get the witness to say something dramatic on the stand. If the system is used properly, the most dramatic thing a witness will say is "yes." Focusing on looking good will immediately mature your cross-examination.

Similarly, by thinking more about form and less about substance, you will not allow yourself to perform a cross-examination involving incantations, begging, or pillaging. You may or may not always elicit some of the information you would like, but you will not engage in meaningless pleasantries, beg, or viciously attack witnesses. Begging and beating up on witnesses looks bad, even if you may occasionally get something substantive out of them. It is not worth making the witness look bad if the price you pay is that you look even worse. Most of the initial incantations we have been taught to use look and sound really stupid. "A foolish consistency is the hobgoblin of little minds"—Ralph Waldo Emerson. By focusing on looking good, we begin to correct some of the bad habits that the conventional wisdom of cross-examination has taught us.

Obtaining helpful information, discrediting witnesses and their testimony, and bolstering the credibility of other witnesses may be worthwhile goals within any given cross-examination, but they are not its primary goals. The underlying premise of my system, and of the rest of this book, is that to be successful in cross-examination, you must strive to look good. Form is more important than substance.

B. THREE HOUSEKEEPING RULES

Rule 1: Almost all courts have lecterns.

They probably belong and, indeed, look good in courtrooms. That said, *a cross-examiner should not stand behind a lectern when cross-examining*, or, for that matter, doing almost anything during a trial with the possible exceptions of addressing the judge or conducting a direct examination.

Why avoid the lectern? Because one cannot and will not properly and effectively communicate from behind one. "If your presentation will be delivered from a lectern, you should experiment. If appropriate, move to the side or front of the lectern to get nearer the audience. Many professional speakers do this. It is engaging, and audiences feel closer to the speaker without barriers." Mandel, *Technical Presentation Skills—A Practical Guide for Better Speaking*, p.55.

Remember the importance of body language. Lecterns effectively cover, at the very least, the lower part of your body. Actually, they usually cover the bottom two-thirds of your body. So much for body language.

Watch the preachers on Sunday T.V. By and large, they are outstanding communicators. You will notice that in recent years many have gone to a glass lectern, one you can see through. Why? Because they know the importance of body language. They might read the Bible to you from behind the lectern, but when it comes to the main message, when they are asking you for money, they do not hide behind a lectern. They understand how to communicate.

A few lawyers complain that their judge requires them to use the lectern. Very few, as the requirement is deservedly going out like starched underwear. Obviously, I have no control over this problem. I do, however, suggest that those of you beset with this problem consider the "touch rule." Try standing very close to but not behind the lectern. Stand close enough to the lectern to rest your hand on it. This usually satisfies the few remaining lectern judges: "See, judge, I am touching it."

Rule 2: Notes can be a problem if not treated properly.
I have taught with several excellent trial advocacy instructors who, when a participant gets up to address the jury or a witness, initially distract the young lawyer and use this distraction to take their notes. The point these instructors are making—they do not want the lawyer using notes—is well taken, though the remedy is a bit harsh and probably overdone.

Again, our reference is communication. Paramount to effective communication is eye contact with those with whom we wish to communicate. A person reading from notes cannot have the required eye contact.

Personally, I have no problem with trial lawyers having notes—as long as they do not *read* from them to the jury. Having important names, dates or phrases, for instance, may be not only helpful but often necessary. When you need to refer to these notes, you may *briefly* do so. While doing so, do not continue to talk to the jury. Read what you must, and then, with eye contact, make your point to the jury.

Rule 3: When communicating, do not hold a writing instrument in your hand.

How often have you seen a lawyer conduct a cross-examination (or, even more often, a direct examination) while holding a pen or pencil? Writing instruments or, for that matter, almost anything that serves no purpose are distractions to communications.[2]

In their defense, a few younger lawyers have argued that they need to write down important things that are said. My response is, if it is so important, then write it down for everyone, especially the jury, to see. How about using a blackboard? I am aware of the many sophisticated exhibits or demonstration aids that are now available. Still, I have a preference for the old-fashioned blackboard. Admittedly, this could be in part because of my own limitations and shortcomings when it comes to modern technology.

Most of us spent our early formative years learning from all-knowing teachers who used the blackboard. What they wrote on the blackboard was the word of God. Those years of inhaling chalk dust have left a lasting and powerful impression. So if the witness says something important, write it on the blackboard. This applies to both cross- and direct examination.

Some lawyers who have practiced for many years have questioned my suggestion to write on a blackboard during cross- (or direct) examination. "What are the foundation requirements?," they ask. The requirement is simple. Anything the witness says can be written on a blackboard and, for that matter, usually anything you say, particularly on cross-examination.

> "[C]ross-examination in a technical area frequently requires the availability of material or at least effective demonstrative aids."
>
> *Thermo King Corporation v. White's Trucking Service, Inc.* 292 F.2d 668, 676 (5th Cir. 1961)

> "No permission or foundation is needed for a lawyer to write on a blackboard as the examination proceeds, so long as what

2. In more recent years I have been disappointed by the number of news communicators who wield writing instruments.

is written is drawn from either a proper question or a proper answer."

Siemer, *Tangible Evidence: How to Use Exhibits at Trial* (2d ed. 1989)

The blackboard itself is not usually admissible in evidence and, accordingly, does not go back to the jury. But that was not and is not your intention.

C. PRIMACY AND RECENCY

Every good trial advocacy program, and there are many, emphasizes the importance of primacy and recency in trying cases. They emphasize these important concepts as they apply to opening statements and closing arguments. Always start with an important and positive theme and, likewise, end with one. These will be the things best remembered.

However, for some reason I have never understood, these important communication concepts are not usually associated with cross- or direct examination. They should be. By not considering and emphasizing these concepts, the teaching of both cross and direct suffers.

As mentioned earlier, most trial lawyers, as indeed I did for many years, start cross-examination with a salutation. We also like to introduce ourselves.[3] We greet the witness, almost always by name. In the words of a long-deceased trial lawyer, we "slather them up and slather them down." ["Good morning, Mrs. Jones. I hope you had a pleasant trip to the courthouse this morning. Let me introduce myself, I am Terry MacCarthy. Now, if you do not hear or understand me, you just stop me and let me know. This will not take long, I just have a few questions. Would you like some coffee and a donut before we get started?"] OK, this last one we do not use, probably because we never thought about it.

---

3. Before introducing yourself or greeting the witness, you would be well advised to check the judge's local rules. Federal District Court Judge Philip G. Reinhard, who sits in Rockford, Illinois (the Western Division of the Northern District of Illinois), specifically admonishes lawyers not to "greet or introduce" themselves to "adverse witnesses." Judge Reinhard's *Trial Procedures—Trial Behavior*.

These archaic, ritualistic incantations hurt rather than help our cause. A communicator, which is what a trial lawyer is and should aspire to be, must always apply the concepts of primacy and recency to all we do as trial lawyers. Recall mention of the Duke Study[4] and the fact that jurors are understandably turned off by meaningless salutations—another good reason to do something different. They want you to be a professional and start like a lawyer with a message. That something will then be primacy.

All teachers of trial advocacy emphasize the importance of having a "theory of the case." Obviously, a theory of the case is necessary. But how important is it? For most cases, the theory is transparently obvious. Of more significance and importance to me are the "themes" in the case. What good facts do you have going for you, and what are your bad facts? Most trial cases will have both. The good facts are the good themes. The bad facts are the bad themes. Your trial story line will emphasize the good themes but also acknowledge, while "sugar coating," the bad themes. From those "good themes" or from available impeaching material, you will create the primacy you will use in cross-examining a witness.

Let us apply primacy to cross-examination. Consider the relatively simple mugging case. A woman leaves the Chug-a-lug Bar around midnight. She has a three-block walk to get home. The second block requires her to walk under a viaduct or overpass. Though lights were originally installed under the overpass, the neighborhood kids took much enjoyment in shooting them out. It is dark under the overpass, where she is robbed.

On direct examination, the woman points to your Johnny and unequivocally states that he was the man who mugged her and stole her purse. Indeed, "she would never forget the face." You probably do not like these facts—the bad themes—but you now must cross-examine.

We want to and will start with primacy. What, then, are the good themes? This is an eyewitness identification case, and it was dark when the woman saw her mugger. This is the one we will use to demonstrate primacy.

---

4. *See* William M. O'Barr, Linguistic Evidence, Language, Power and Strategy in the Courtroom (1982) (reporting the work of the Law and Language Project at Duke University, which studied various aspects of communication and linguistic courtroom behaviors and their effects on jurors).

Other good themes might be: she had been drinking in the Chug-a-Lug Bar for several hours; it is a cross-racial identification; and finally, and usually most important, her description of the mugger will not totally fit your Johnny, even if he was the mugger.

As mentioned, we will use the "it was dark" theme for primacy. We will start our cross, after a brief pause:[5]

Attorney: It is fair to say it was dark out that night?

We start every cross-examination with one of these three phrases:

1. "It is fair to say . . ."
2. "We can agree . . ."
3. "The fact is . . ." or "The truth is . . . ."

I have a strong preference for the first two.

Wait a minute, might not "we can agree" be objectionable? It could be argued, though I have never heard of this objection being made, that what the cross-examiner and witness "agree on" is irrelevant. If this stupid objection is ever made, there is a good chance that it might be sustained. So what? This is what will happen.

Attorney (on cross): We can agree it was dark out that night?
Opposing Attorney: Objection. Whether counsel agrees or not is irrelevant.
Court: Sustained.
Attorney (on cross): It was dark out that night?
Witness: Yes.

This is but one of many examples where an objection, though it may be legally proper, will make the objecting lawyer look bad. Surely there are better and more powerful examples of primacy. The one we used, "dark out," is thematic. Often our primacy will be thematic. But another wonderful source of primacy remains: impeachment, the weapon of mass destruction.

5. The communicative pause, a brief one, should be used at the start and when you have completed your cross. Watch, for instance, the old episodes of *L.A. Law* and you will usually see this done to perfection.

nal favorite is usually available only to those of us who ... criminal cases. How is this for impactive primacy?

Attorney: We can agree you are a convicted felon?[6]

You cannot improve on this.

In cross-examining a "snitch," you could start with: "You would do almost anything not to go back to jail."

OK, so you try civil cases and do not get to cross-examine many, if any, convicted felons or "snitches." How about something like this:

Attorney: We can agree you are a liar?

Obviously, this would require your being able to properly impeach the witness with Federal Rule of Evidence 608(B). Do you have an instance or, even better, instances when the witness lied or was untruthful? More probably you would at least have the following available to you:

Attorney: We can agree you work for the defendant's corporation?

Obviously, this is "motivation" impeachment. It has less impact but still serves our desire to use primacy.

In sum, primacy often will be predicated upon proper impeachment. Other times your primacy will be thematic, as illustrated by our ". . . it was dark . . ." example. Whatever the source, use primacy and avoid the condescending salutations.

A final point: Unlike those who use the condescending salutations to start their cross-examinations, we will *not* call the witness by

6. There is still another rule of trial advocacy and storytelling. Every person who is important to your case and your story should have a "label." Most readers of a book or listeners to any complex story get confused with names. They forget them or, at the very least, forget who was who. The simple distinction between the "tall" and the "short" police officers, or the "officer with the mustache," rather than their respective names, helps our ability to communicate. Use descriptive labels rather than names. Add to this communication rule the bonus points you will receive when, as above, the "label" you will be using is that of "convicted felon."

name or use an honorific. Get rid of the "Mrs. Jones," "doctor," "sergeant" references. The use of these appellations empowers the witness and makes him or her less subject to the control we want during cross-examination.[7]

Though this is obvious common sense, I was first made aware of it when I had the honor of serving on the police board of the village where we raised our family. An outside corporation, using experienced experts, interviewed aspiring police officers. This is a common and accepted practice. They know what they are doing, and by and large do a good job. To enhance the control they want (I confess I never fully understood why they wanted control), those doing the interviews do not refer to those being interviewed by name. Instead, they would have them sit on a chair with a designated color. When spoken to or questioned, candidates were addressed by the color of their chair.

A few have questioned me on this suggestion. "If we cannot call them by name, what do we call them?" You call them nothing. There is no need or reason to use someone's name (unless, of course, it is an issue) when cross-examining.

Recency

As we want to start on a high note, so also do we want to end on a high note. This is what we mean by recency.

This requirement often poses problems for public defenders. Return to the mugging case. Assume, as (unfortunately for us) it is often the case, that the woman is not a drinker, there is no cross-racial identification, and, though indeed highly questionable, her description matches Johnny in every respect. We still have "it was dark" as our primacy, but we have nothing different for recency. Accept your unfortunate limitations. Your recency, already familiar to the jury, will be: "It was dark under the overpass?"

When I think of the recency requirement, I think of one of Professor Younger's Ten Commandments of Cross-Examination. His somewhat related commandment is, "Do not ask the one question too many." A few who have heard my talk have suggested that his

---

7. There will be one exception to this rule. It will come toward the end of the book, when we talk about how to handle and "tweak" the intractable witness during cross-examination.

commandment and my concept of recency are basically telling us the same thing. Believe me, they are anything but the same thing. Younger used illustrations and stories second to none. They, befitting the great storyteller that he was, were poignant and painted vivid pictures—pictures you were not soon to forget. Unfortunately, on a few occasions, the pictures created were somewhat misleading.

The "one question too many" example comes to mind. First off, the commandment, when you think about it, is basically useless to the cross-examining trial lawyer because we are not told when or how we will know which question is the "one question too many." Younger's example, while illustrative of his skill as a storyteller, in truth makes no sense to the trial lawyer.

You will recall the infamous "nose bite" case. No less than Abraham Lincoln was the criminal defense lawyer. He cross-examined the prosecutor's witness. Initially he brought out that the witness was birdwatching. A good theme, but again, a relatively weak criminal defense theme. He was using what he had.

Then Lincoln suggested to the witness that, in fact, he, the witness, had not seen the defendant bite off the poor fellow's nose. The witness agreed. We are told by Younger that Lincoln should then have stopped and sat down. But he continued and violated the commandment against asking the one question too many. Lincoln's last question to the witness, the one question too many, was: "So if you did not see him bite the nose off, how do you know he bit it off?"

The witness answer sticks with us: "I saw him spit it out."

A great story. The story is so good it covers up the trial advocacy shortcomings and problems. First off, and we will cover this in more detail later, Lincoln used an open-ended question. This, as you will learn, should never be done on cross-examination. Next, and more significantly, accepting Younger's teaching, Lincoln should have simply stopped after establishing that the witness did not see the nose being bitten off. This sounds good and certainly makes the point for the "one question too many" commandment. Unfortunately, it makes no sense to the trial lawyer, who realizes that after Lincoln's cross, the prosecutor gets to redirect the witness.

Assuming Lincoln had, as suggested by Younger, stopped the cross short of the one question too many, the first question by the prosecutor on redirect would have been: "If you did not see the defendant bite off the nose, how do you know he bit it off?" Here, on direct, the open-ended question is permissible, proper, and persuasive. Therefore, in the first instance, where Lincoln asked the "one question too many," he came off looking dumb. In the second instance, where Lincoln observed the commandment and it was left to the prosecutor to bring out the totally impactive information, Lincoln not only looked dumb but, far more significantly, he lost his credibility.

When concluding a cross, end on a positive or high note. This will never happen with an open-ended question.

Attachment A

Cross-examination of Dr. Kumagai from
Presumed Innocent, by Scott Turow.
Used with permission of the author.

"Doc-tor Kumagai," Stern begins, "you have testified here as an expert, is that right?"

"Yes, sir."

"You have told us about your papers and your degrees, have you not?"

"I answer questions about that, yes."

"You said you have testified on many prior occasions."

"Hundreds," says Painless. Each answer has a kind of screw-you brittleness. He means to be a smart guy and tough, the better of any cross-examiner.

"Doctor, has your competence ever been called into question, to your knowledge?"

Painless adjusts himself on the stand. The assault has begun. "No, sir," he says.

"Doctor, is it not true that many deputy prosecuting attorneys over the years have complained about your competence as a forensic pathologist?"

"Not to me."

"No, not to you. But to the chief of police, resulting in at least one memorandum being placed in your personnel file?"

"I don't know about that."

Sandy shows the document first to Nico, then to Kumagai on the stand.

"No, I never seen that," he says at once.

"Do you not have to be notified under police regulations of any addition to your personnel file?"

"Could be, but you ask what I remember. I don't remember that."

"Thank you, Doctor." Sandy removes the document from Kumagai's hands. As Stern is strolling back to our table, he asks, "Do you have any nicknames?"

Kumagai stills. Perhaps he is wishing that he had acknowledged the letter.

"Friend call me Ted."

"Aside from that?"

"Don't use nicknames."

"No, sir, not that you use. But by which you are known?"

"I don't understand question."

"Has anybody ever referred to you as Painless?"

"To me?"

"To anyone, to your knowledge?"

Again Painless takes a moment to shift around in his seat.

"Could be," he says finally.

"You do not enjoy that nickname, do you?"

"Don't think about it."

"You acquired that nickname some years ago from the former chief deputy prosecuting attorney Mr. Sennett, in an unflattering context, did you not?"

"If you say."

"Mr. Sennett told you to your face, did he not, that *you* had bungled an autopsy and that the only person who found working with you painless was the corpse, because it was dead?"

The laughter thunders in the courtroom. Even Lanen is chuckling up on the bench. I shift in my seat. Whatever Stern has better be good, because for the first time he has abandoned his innate decorousness. His cross so far verges on the cruel.

"I don't remember that," says Painless coldly when the room has come back to order again. Over the years he has grown adroit in his knowledge of the rules of evidence. Every cop and P.A. in Kindle County knows that story. Stan Sennett would be happy to tell it from the stand. But the judge is not likely to allow such a diversion, called collateral impeachment. Painless has drawn his shoulders around him. He looks out at Stern, waiting for more. He has apparently taken some pleasure in what he regards as his own small triumph.

"Now, Mr. Della Guardia and Mr. Molto are two persons from the P.A.'s office with whom you have worked with less—let us say disagreement, is that right?"

"Sure. They my good friends." On this point, Painless has apparently been well schooled. He will acknowledge his contacts with Tommy and Delay, in order to minimize their importance.

"Did you discuss this investigation with either one of them while it was in progress?"

"I talk to Mr. Molto sometime."

"How often did you speak to him?"

"We stay in touch. We talk now and then."

"Did you talk to him more than five times in the first few weeks of April?"

"Sure," he says, "if you say." Painless is taking no chances.

He knows that subpoenas are out. He can't be sure whose MUDs we have obtained.

"And you talked in detail about this investigation?"

"Mr. Molto's a friend. He ask what I'm doin. I tell him. We talk about public information. Nothin from the gran jury." Painless resumes his satisfied smile. These answers, of course, have been the subject of prior discussion with the prosecutors.

"Did you tell Mr. Molto the results of the forensic chemist's analysis prior to conveying them to Mr. Sabich? I am talking specifically about the specimen which showed the spermicidal jelly."

"I understand," says Painless curtly. He looks directly over at Tommy. Molto has his hand over part of his face, and with Kumagai's glance, he straightens up and takes it away.

"I think so," says Kumagai.

He has not quite finished his response when Lanen interrupts.

"Just a second," says the judge. "Just *one* second. The record will reflect that Prosecuting Attorney Molto has just made a gesture which I recognize to be a signal to the witness in connection with his last answer. There will be further proceedings with regard to Mr. Molto at a later time. Proceed, Mr. Stern."

Tommy is crimson as he struggles to his feet.

"Your Honor, I am terribly sorry. I don't know what you are talking about."

Neither do I, and I was watching Molto. But Lanen is inflamed.

"This jury is not blind. Mr. Molto. And neither am I. Proceed," he says to Stern, but his anger is too great to store away and he immediately wheels his chair around in Molto's direction and gestures with the gavel. "I warned you. I told you before. I am very upset with your conduct during this trial, Mr. Molto. There will be proceedings."

"Judge," says Tommy despairingly.

"Resume your seat, sir. Mr. Stern, proceed."

Stern comes over to the table. I explain what I saw. He, too, observed nothing. But Stern does not let the incident pass. In a mincing tone he asks, "It is fair to say, Dr. Kumagai, that you and Mr. Molto have always had good communication, is it not?"

The question evokes a few snickers, especially from the reporters' section. Kumagai blinks with disdain and fails to answer.

"Dr. Kumagai," asks Stern, "it is your ambition, is it not, sir, to become coroner of Kindle County?"

"I like to be coroner," says Painless with disarmingly little hesitation. "Dr. Russell doin a good job now. Couple years he retire, maybe I put in for the job."

"And the P.A.'s recommendation would help you obtain that position, would it not?"

"Who knows?" Painless smiles. "Can't hurt."

Grudgingly, I must admire Delay. Kumagai is his witness and he has obviously counseled him to play it straight about whatever was going on during the election campaign. Nico quite clearly wants to have some prosecutorial candor to troop before the jury to make up for some of Molto's gaffes. And his judgment strikes me as correct. If it were not for the incident with the judge a moment ago, it would all sit pretty well.

"By April, had you and Mr. Molto ever discussed the possibility of you becoming coroner, Dr. Kumagai?"

"I say. Mr. Molto and me friends. I talk about what I wanna do, he talk about what he wanna do. Talk all the time. April. May. June."

"And in April you also spoke about this investigation a number of times before you received the forensic chemist's report?"

"I'd say so."

"Now, that report, sir, concerned the semen specimen which you had taken from Ms. Polhemus during the autopsy, is that right?"

"Right. "

"And it is that specimen which has been identified as being of Mr. Sabich's blood type and as containing chemicals consistent with the use by Ms. Polhemus of a birth-control device—a diaphragm. Am I correct?"

"You are correct."

"And the presence in that specimen of this birth-control chemical, the spermicide, is critical to your opinion, is it not?"

"All facts important, Mr. Stern."

"But that fact is particularly important, because you, sir, want us to believe that this tragic incident merely had the appearance of a rape, do you not?"

"Don't want you to believe nothin. I give you my opinion."

"But it is your opinion—to get down to brass tacks, as they say—that Mr. Sabich tried to make this look like a rape, correct?"

"If you say so."

"Well, is that not what you are trying to suggest? You and Mr. Molto, and Mr. Della Guardia? Let us be plain with these people." Sandy points to the jury. "Your opinion is that this was a staged rape.

And that the way it was done suggests some knowledge of investigative techniques and of Ms. Polhemus's regular duties in the P.A.'s office, correct?"

"That's what I say on direct."

"And all of that points at Mr. Sabich, does it not?"

"If you say so," Painless says eventually, with a smile. You can see his reluctance to believe that Stern is inept enough to implicate his own client. But Sandy keeps forcing the issue, saying more than Kumagai would risk on his own, and Painless takes his characteristic pleasure in someone else's misfortune.

"And all those deductions depend in the end on the presence of spermicidal jelly in the specimen you sent to the forensic chemist, do they not?"

"More or less."

"Much more than less, is it not?"

"I would say."

"So this specimen, and the presence of the spermicide, is critical to your expert opinion?" says Stern, arriving at the point where he was a moment ago. This time Painless concedes. He shrugs his shoulders and says all right.

"Now, does your expert opinion, Dr. Kumagai, take any account of the fact that no spermicidal jelly was found in Ms. Polhemus's apartment? Are you familiar with that testimony that was given here by Detective Greer?"

"My opinion on scientific evidence. I don't read the transcript."

"But are you familiar with that testimony?"

"I heard about it."

"And are you not concerned, as an expert, that your opinion depends on the presence of a substance not found in the victim's belongings?"

"Am I concerned?"

"That is my question."

"Not concerned. I got an opinion on scientific evidence." Stern gives Painless the long look.

"Spermicide came from somewhere, Mr. Stern. I don't know where lady hides this stuff. It's in the specimen. Test says what it says."

"Just so," says Sandy Stern.

"You stipulated," says Kumagai.

"That the spermicide was in the specimen you sent. Yes, sir, we did agree to that." Sandy walks around the courtroom. I still cannot guess what it is that Kumagai missed. Until Painless mentioned the stipulation I was ready to bet that the spermicide was misidentified.

"Now, sir," says Stern, "your initial impressions at the time of the autopsy took no account of the presence of a spermicide, did they?"

"Can't remember now."

"Well, think back, please. Was it not your original theory that the person who had last had intercourse with Ms. Polhemus was sterile?"

"Don't recall."

"Really? You told Detective Lipranzer that Ms. Polhemus's attacker seemed to have a condition in which he produced dead spermatozoa, did you not? Detective Lipranzer has already testified once before the jury, I am sure it would be no problem for him to return. Please reflect, Dr. Kumagai, is that not what you said?"

"Maybe. Very preliminary."

"All right, it was your very preliminary opinion. But it was your opinion then?"

"I guess."

"Now, do you recall the physical findings that led you to that opinion?"

"No, sir."

"As a matter of fact, Doctor, I am sure it is difficult for you to recall, unaided, any autopsy within days of when it took place, is that right?"

"Sometime. "

"How many autopsies do you do in a week, Dr. Kumagai?"

"One, two. Sometime ten. Depends."

"Do you remember how many you performed in the thirty days surrounding Carolyn Polhemus's death?"

"No, sir,"

"Would you be surprised to know that it was eighteen?"

"Sound right."

"And with that number, it is obvious, is it not, that the specifics of any one examination may slip your mind?"

"True."

"But when you spoke to Lipranzer the details were fresher. Were they not?"

"Probably."

"And you told him then that you believed the attacker was sterile?"

"I say. I somewhat remember that."

"Well, let us review for a moment those findings you presently recall that might have led to that preliminary opinion."

Sandy runs through it quickly. The rigor mortis, blood coagulation, and digestive enzymes established the time of death. The primary deposit of male fluids in the rear of the vagina, away from the vulva, indicated that Carolyn had spent little time on her feet after sex, meaning that intercourse had occurred near the time of her attack. And there was an absence in the fallopian tubes of any live spermatozoa, which one would expect to find ten to twelve hours after intercourse, assuming no contraception had been used.

"And to explain these phenomena, particularly the dead spermatozoa, you theorized that the attacker was sterile. It did not occur to you at first, Doctor, that a spermicide had been used, did it?"

"Apparently not."

"As you look back, you must think you were a fool to have missed something so obvious as the use of a contraceptive spermicide?"

"Make mistakes," allows Painless with a flip of his hand.

"You do?" asks Stern. He eyes the state's expert. "How often?" Kumagai does not answer that. He recognizes his miscue.

"Mr. Stern, I find no birth-control device. No diaphragm. Apparently, I assume no birth control used."

"But certainly, Dr. Kumagai, an expert of your stature could not have been so easily misled?"

Kumagai smiles. He knows he is being taunted.

"Any single fact important," he says. "Kind of thing that murderer knows."

"But you yourself were not trying to mislead Detective Lipranzer when you gave him your initial impression, were you?"

"Oh no." Painless shakes his head vigorously. He has been prepared for that suggestion.

"You must have been convinced, Doctor, at that time, that birth control had not been used—so convinced that you considered the use of a spermicide to be out of the question?"

"Look, Mr. Stern." I got an opinion. Chemist has results. Opinion changes. Lipranzer know opinion's preliminary."

"Let us consider some alternatives. For example, Dr. Kumagai, you would be convinced that birth control would not be used by a woman who knew she could not bear children, correct?"

"Sure," he says. "But Ms. Polhemus got a child."

"So the evidence has shown," remarks Stern. "But let us not consider the particulars of Ms. Polhemus. Just bear my example in mind. If a woman knew she could not conceive, it would be unreasonable for her to use a spermicide, would it not?"

"Sure. Unreasonable," Painless agrees, but his answers are growing slower. His eyes seem thick. He has no idea where Stern is headed.

"Absurd?"

"I'd say."

"Can you, as a forensic expert, conceive of any reason that such a woman might use a diaphragm or a spermicide?"

"We not talkin about a lady in menopause?"

"We are speaking of a woman who knows without question that she cannot conceive."

"No reason. No medical reason. I think of nothin."

Sandy looks up at Lanen. "Your honor, may the court reporter mark the last five questions and answers so that she can read them back later, if need be?"

Kumagai conducts a slow survey of the courtroom. He looks at the judge, the reporter, finally the prosecutors' table. He is actually frowning now. The trap, whatever it is, has been set. Everyone knows it. The reporter attaches a clip to the narrow sheaf of stenographic notes.

"Is it not your expert opinion, Dr. Kumagai," asks my lawyer, Alejandro Stern, "that Carolyn Polhemus was a woman who knew she could not conceive?"

Kumagai looks out at Stern. He bends over the microphone before the witness chair.

"No," Painless says.

"Please do not rush yourself, Doctor. You did eighteen autopsies in those weeks. Would you not rather consider your original notes?"

""I know the lady use birth control. You stipulate," he says again.

"And I, sir, say once more that we stipulated to the chemist's identification of the specimen that you sent."

Stern returns to our table. Kemp is already holding aloft the document Sandy wants. Stern drops a copy with the prosecution and delivers the original to Kumagai.

"Do you recognize the notes of your autopsy of Ms. Polhemus, Dr. Kumagai?"

Painless flips a few pages.

"My signature," he says.

"Would you please read aloud the short passage marked by the paper clip?" Sandy turns to Nico. "Page 2, Counsel."

Kumagai has to change glasses.

"'The fallopian tubes are ligated and separated. The fimbriated ends appear normal.'" Kumagai looks down at the sheet he has read from. He pages again to the end. He is frowning, deeply now.

Finally he shakes his head.

"Not right," he says.

"Your own autopsy notes? You dictate them as you are conducting the procedure, do you not? Surely, Doctor, you are not suggesting you made a contemporaneous error?"

"Not right," he says again.

Stern comes back to the defense table for another piece of paper. I have gotten it by now. I look up to him as he takes the next document from Kemp. I whisper:

"Are you telling me that Carolyn Polhemus had her tubes tied?"

It is Kemp who nods.

The next few seconds are blank. Weirdly, unaccountably, I feel alone, locked in my own teetering sensations. An essential connection has been interrupted. For a moment it is like déjà vu. I cannot make out reasons. What takes place in the courtroom seems remote. I am aware, in a dislocated way, that Painless Kumagai is being devastated. He denies two or three more times that it is possible that Ms. Polhemus had had her fallopian tubes surgically separated to prevent conception. Stern asks if other facts might affect his opinion and pushes into Kumagai's hands the records of the West End gynecologist who performed the tubal ligation six and a half years ago, after Carolyn aborted a pregnancy. It was this doctor, no doubt, whom Kemp went to meet yesterday afternoon.

"I ask you again, sir, would these records alter your expert opinion?"

Kumagai does not answer.

"Sir, is it now your expert opinion that Carolyn Polhemus knew she could not conceive?"

"Apparently." Kumagai looks up from the papers. In my confusion, I find that I actually feel sorry for him. He is slow now, hollow. It is to Molto and Nico he speaks, not Stern or the jury. "I forgot," he tells them.

"Sir, is it not absurd to believe that Carolyn Polhemus used a spermicide on the night of April first?"

Kumagai does not answer.

"Is it not unreasonable to believe that?"

Kumagai does not respond.

"There is no reason known to you that would explain why she might do that, is there, sir?"

Kumagai looks up. There is no way to tell if he is thinking or simply being ravaged by shame. He has taken hold of the beveled rail of the witness stand. He still does not answer.

"Shall I have the court reporter read back your answers to the questions I asked a few moments ago?"

Kumagai shakes his head.

"Is it not clear, Dr. Kumagai, that Carolyn Polhemus did not use a spermicide on April first? Would that not be your expert opinion? Does it not seem to you, sir, as an expert and a scientist, the most obvious reason that no trace of a spermicide could be found in her apartment?"

Kumagai seems to sigh. "I cannot answer your questions, sir," he says with some dignity.

"Well, answer this question, Dr. Kumagai: Is it not clear, given these facts, that the specimen you sent to the chemist was not taken from the body of Carolyn Polhemus?"

Kumagai now sits back. He pushes his glasses back up on his nose.

"I have a regular procedure."

"Are you telling this jury, sir, that you have a clear recollection of taking that specimen, marking it, sending it on?"

"No."

"I repeat: Is it not likely that the specimen containing the spermicide, the specimen identified as containing fluids of Mr. Sabich's blood type, was not taken from the body of Carolyn Polhemus?"

Painless shakes his head again. But this is not denial. He does not know what occurred.

"Sir, is it not likely?"

"It is possible," he finally says.

From the jury box, clear across the courtroom, I can hear one of the men say, "For Chrissake."

"And that specimen, Dr. Kumagai, was sent, was it not, while you were having these regular conversations with Mr. Molto, am I right?"

With this, Kumagai finally rediscovers his spark. He draws himself up in the chair.

"Do you accuse me, Mr. Stern?"

It is some time before Stern speaks.

"We have had enough unsupported accusations for one case," he says. Then, before resuming his chair, Stern nods in the direction of the witness, as if to dismiss him. "Doc-tor Kumagai," he adds.

7 The System, Part I: "Short"

Here is my system for successful cross-examination:

SHORT + STATEMENTS = CONTROL

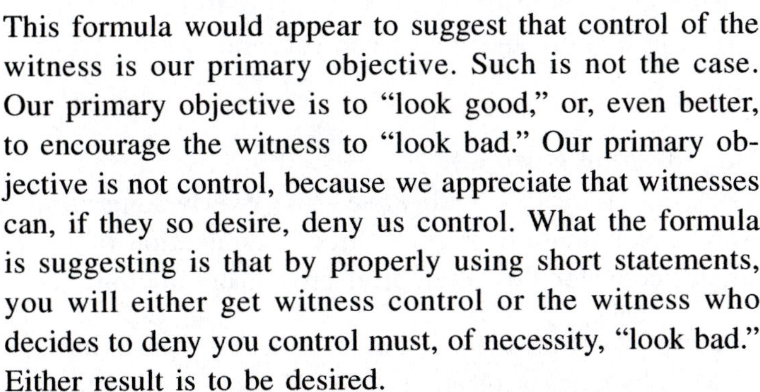

This formula would appear to suggest that control of the witness is our primary objective. Such is not the case. Our primary objective is to "look good," or, even better, to encourage the witness to "look bad." Our primary objective is not control, because we appreciate that witnesses can, if they so desire, deny us control. What the formula is suggesting is that by properly using short statements, you will either get witness control or the witness who decides to deny you control must, of necessity, "look bad." Either result is to be desired.

Most young lawyers with whom I have worked seek and want witness control. More experienced trial lawyers appreciate that if the witness "looks bad," you as the cross-examiner are profiting more than you would have had you merely kept control. This point will be demonstrated when we cover "control" and the intractable witness. Let us talk about the three terms of the formula.

Most who teach cross-examination suggest you should keep it short. Some suggest one fact per question. This phrase is misleading and inaccurate for two reasons. (Yes, I know I should have had three reasons!) First off, a "fact" may be longer than my concept of short—which you will soon see. Second, the suggestion to use a question is not consistent with our system (to be explained later). It is easy to tell a cross-examiner to be short; it would, however, be better to explain *why* he or she should be short.

A. THREE REASONS TO BE SHORT

1. The length of the question (statement) usually determines the length of the answer.

Several years ago, research was conducted to determine what effect the length of a question (yes, they used questions, but their research was not related to trial advocacy) had on the length of the answer. They primarily used press conferences with President Kennedy. Actually, we as trial lawyers could have saved them some time and money by providing them with our transcripts. They concluded—and our transcripts would have supported this—that the length of the question usually, but not always, determines the length of the answer.

This conclusion gives us justification and reason to be short. If we want the witness to be short and under control, and we do, then we must be short.

2. The long question is stupid.

I have witnessed—indeed, we all have—the overly long-winded and legalistic cross-examination or even direct examination of a witness. For example, consider this attempt at cross-examination.

Attorney: Now, Mr. Smith, is it not a fact that you exited Murphy's bar at or about three o'clock in the afternoon and when you exited the bar there was a light rain and you observed a vehicle, and the vehicle you observed was a green Pontiac convertible being driven by a man you knew to be Tom Clancy, and he had a passenger in the front seat, a blonde woman whom you did not know and his vehicle was going west on Adams, isn't that correct?

Witness: No.

The problem, of course, is that the attorney does not know to which one of his many questions the witness has answered "no." The cross-examiner has laid out a long sausage. Now he must get a sharp knife and cut the long sausage into small pieces. The witness also knows what has happened and, given the opportunity, may well attempt to explain his or her answer.

3. You will be less likely to look bad.

The third reason to be short is that you are less likely to screw up. Keeping it short minimizes the opportunity for the witness to hurt you. Besides, you will sound better, be in better control of your story, and leave everybody, including yourself, less confused.

B. HOW SHORT CAN YOU MAKE YOUR CROSS-EXAMINATION?

How short—how few words—can you make your cross-examination statement? At this point in my lecture, I ask the audience how short *they* think we can get our cross-examination. I select the person who has suggested the greatest number—let us say five words. I then explain that the answer is one. Indeed, many who have heard my lecture and use my system call it "one-word cross."

Thomas Jefferson would be proud. He is quoted as saying, "The most valuable of all talents is that of never using two words when one will do." Also, George Orwell told us: "If it is possible to cut a word out, always cut it out." [*Politics and the English Language, Collected Essays, Journalism and Letters of George Orwell*, vol. 4 (1968), at 127, 139.] Also William Strunk, Jr., and E. B. White tell us, in *The Elements of Style* [Macmillan, 3rd edition, 1979], "Omit needless words."

Ostensibly to prove my point, I go about demonstrating my ability to cross with one word. I use as the witness the participant who suggested five as the answer. I direct my cross to that person and simply say "green." I get little or no response and certainly not the desired "yes." The audience laughs—not with me, but at me. To say the least, this gets their attention and allows me to explain how to do "one-word cross."

C. HOW TO MAKE YOUR CROSS-EXAMINATION SHORT

1. Eliminate the prefixes. (*Isn't it a fact you went to the store?)*
2. Eliminate the suffixes. (*You went to the store, isn't that correct?)*
3. Use TRANSITIONS.

The reasons and justification for 1 and 2 above, the elimination of traditional leading phrases, are explained later. Transitions are covered next.

D. TRANSITIONS

There is no trial advocacy tool more helpful, more necessary, and more communicative than the transition, particularly during direct or cross-examination. Open your "trial advocacy toolbox" and you will find the transition tool. It is a good tool to use in voir dire, openings, and closings. It is absolutely necessary during cross-examination and exceptionally helpful on direct examination.

> Good transitions are useful to the audience because they make clear the thought patterns of the speaker and the relationship of evidence to the conclusion it supports. In the form of internal summaries, good transitions aid memory, recall, and understanding of the speaker's material. [Minnick, *Public Speaking*, p. 84.]

Anyone who has ever put a witness on the stand on direct examination has used a transition. The traditional, standard, but unfortunately archaic transition goes something like this. "Mr. Witness, calling your attention to June 10, 2004, at or about 3:00 p.m., while you were in Murphy's Bar, what, if anything, unusual occurred?" If you were to recite this convoluted mess to a group of trial lawyers outside a courtroom, as I often have, the reaction would be light laughter, light only because they know they are laughing at themselves. The problem, of course, is that those laughing have used this transition and for the most part continue to use it. Why? Because that is how we were taught—that is what we had to say to prove we were trial lawyers. Unfortunately, most are unaware of the wonderful alternative to the Chesterfieldian formalism transition.

Parenthetically, you may wonder about the origin of the convoluted transition. Although its origin cannot be determined with unquestioned accuracy, the probability is it was created by prosecutors. No, not current prosecutors, though they use it and are the cause of others using it. The prosecutors who created this archaic transition were probably those who prosecuted during the time of Shakespeare. The language certainly suggests this conclusion.

In fairness, prosecutors, old or new, are not totally responsible for the traditional transition. Evidence teachers had an input. They (who else?) added the "if anything." They added this language to make the traditional transition less objectionable. It did. However, it was not objectionable without this additional phrase. One can only conclude that some evidence teachers wear both braces and a belt.

Enough history—let us talk about correcting and changing it, about moving into the twenty-first century. This suggestion of a good and serviceable transition is, in my opinion, my greatest gift to you as a trial lawyer.

> I want to ask you some questions about what you saw when you left Murphy's Bar about 3 in the afternoon, you understand.

If you prefer, you may omit the term "some questions."

This sounds much better. It is consistent with my Rule 11 of Trial Advocacy: "You speak in a courtroom the way you speak in a bar." I have in mind a nice bar, one with carpeting, as distinct from those often frequented by my fellow defenders—those with sawdust on the floor.

Let's apply the Rule 11 litmus test. What would happen if you went up to someone in a bar and said, "Calling your attention to at or about one hour earlier, at or about 4:00 p.m. in the afternoon, what, if anything unusual, occurred in this bar?" Your barroom companion would, in all probability, write you off as a deranged person and seek to escape from you. Conversely, you would not offend or suggest a diminished mental capacity were you to simply say, "I want to ask you about what you saw in this bar an hour ago."

If you were to use this language, you would not bore or aggravate the other person. Therefore, this is the language you should carry into the courtroom.

There are a couple of other related suggestions or observations. The first suggestion introduces another MacCarthy Rule of Trial Advocacy, Rule 37. To be a better trial lawyer, you must learn to use your head. I am not requesting too much of you. I am not asking you to think. Simply stated, all I want you to do is learn to move your head up and down. This body language is powerful. When you move your head up and down while making a statement, the other person to whom you are talking, the witness, and even a judge will move their head up and down with you, which sends a strong message of agreement. Also, with his head going up and down, it is difficult for the person to respond with a negative. You can test this rule in everyday life. Checking into a hotel: "You have a good room for me." Talking to a restaurant maître d': "You have a good table for us."

Note the fiinal two terms of the transition: "you understand." They are important in that you are not asking a question. As explained later, you will get a "yes." Also, this phrase sounds fair and helps protect against an objection.

This transition can and indeed should be used during direct as well as cross-examination. A slight wording change is required, however. To the final terms you must add an extra word: "*do* you understand." Adding "do" satisfies the requirement that you ask questions on direct examination.

Finally, might your cross-examination transition be objected to? Under certain circumstances, yes. Assume the witness, neither on direct nor so far on cross-examination, has mentioned being in Murphy's Bar. An objection that there is no evidence or foundation would be proper and most probably sustained. Of course, you could avoid this by simply telling the witness, "You were in Murphy's Bar on June 10th." Then again, you might handle this differently. Let us see what will happen if you fail to lay the proper foundation.

Q: I want to ask you what you saw when on June 10th you left Murphy's Bar at 3:00 in the afternoon, you understand?
Objection: Your Honor, I object. There is no foundation for this question; more specifically, there is no evidence the witness was ever in Murphy's Bar.
Judge: Sustained.
Q: You have been in Murphy's Bar?
A: Yes.
Q: You were there on June 10?
A: Yes.
Q: You left Murphy's Bar around 3:00 in the afternoon?
A: Yes.

You may want to direct this next statement more toward the objector than the witness.

Q: I want to ask you what you saw when on June 10th you left Murphy's Bar at 3:00 in the afternoon.

Experience working with trial lawyers suggests an additional suggestion or observation. Some lawyers are now properly using the transition but fail to appreciate what they have done. An example best makes this point.

Q: I want to ask you some questions about what you saw and did when you left Lynch's Bar.
A: OK.
Q: You left Lynch's Bar around eight in the evening?
A: Yes.

After using a perfect transition, the second reference to Lynch's Bar is unnecessary and redundant. The question should have been:

Q: That was around eight in the evening?

E. EXAMPLE OF CROSS-EXAMINATION USING THE SYSTEM

Let us now do the Murphy's Bar cross-examination using the system.[1]

Attorney: (a transition) I want to ask you some questions about what you saw when you left Murphy's Bar at 3:00 p.m., you understand?
Witness: Yes.
Attorney: You walked outside?[2]
Witness: Yes.
Attorney: Toward Adams Street?

1. Note the one-word cross.
2. Understand, you are not merely reading a script; rather, you are painting a picture by using body language to act out. For instance, the left hand can show the walking motion.

Witness: Yes.
Witness: You looked around?[3] (This is a "plausibility" statement, albeit not an important one. This will be explained later).
Witness: Yes.
Attorney: There was a light rain falling?[4]
Witness: Yes.
Attorney: You saw a car?
Witness: Yes.
Attorney: A Pontiac?
Witness: Yes.
Attorney: Convertible?
Witness: Yes.
Attorney: Green?
Witness: Yes.
Attorney: You knew the driver?
Witness: Yes.
Attorney: Clancy was driving?
Witness: Yes.
Attorney: Tom Clancy?
Witness: Yes.
Attorney: There was a passenger in the car?
Witness: Yes.
Attorney: A woman?
Witness: Yes.
Attorney: A blonde woman?
Witness: Yes.
Attorney: You did not know her?
Witness: No.
Attorney: The car was going west?
Witness: Yes.
Attorney: On Adams Street?
Witness: Yes.

3. Actually look around as you use the words.
4. Pull your hands down slowly to show the light rain.

We are ready, probably overdue, for another transition.

Attorney: I want to ask you some questions about the next time you saw the car, two hours later, about five o'clock, you understand?
Witness: Yes.
Attorney: Clancy was still driving?
Witness: Yes.
Attorney: You did not see a passenger in the car?[5]
Witness: No.
Attorney: You did not see the blonde woman?
Witness: No.
Attorney: The car was now going east?
Witness: Yes.

Now we continue with another transition.

What we are doing, of course, is telling a story. You should remember to start by saying to yourself these magic words: "once upon a time." This should help launch you into the storytelling mode.

F. LOOPING

We are seeking short storytelling statements, even as short as one word. Still there is, as with most rules, an exception. This exception allows us to get a little longer, to add a few more words, but only with a proper storytelling purpose.

Trial lawyers are, first and foremost, communicators. Communicators know that not everything that is said is of equal importance. Storytelling facts are not equal. We, as communicating trial lawyers, know that usually our audience quickly forgets much of what it has heard. Finally, we know there are terms or themes that are extremely important to the story we are telling. These are the terms or themes that we want the jury or triers of fact to remember. How do we help them remember what we deem important?

5. Note the language selection. If instead you had said, "The blonde woman was not in the car?" the witness, albeit not particularly looking good, could have responded: "She could have been in the car, possibly on the floor, but I did not see her."

As a young lawyer, less concerned with communications and more concerned with proving I was a "real" trial lawyer, which I was not, I tried many cases with older, far more experienced lawyers. Some of them, I always felt, were more concerned with communications than with what others thought of them. Aware of the importance of emphasizing critical facts, they, totally lacking elegance, would tell the witness who had just said something good that they could not hear all that well and ask the witness to repeat what she said. Interestingly, this confession of poor hearing was never made when the witness said something negative. The method was lacking, but the intention was good.

If we were British barristers, we would have no problem. We could and would simply repeat the important declaration to the jury. (We would be talking only about criminal cases in the revered Old Bailey, since juries have been all but been eliminated in civil trials.) Though in our adoption of the common law we took and gained much, we did not adopt the practice of repeating the witness's testimony. But it is interesting to note that movie and TV producers, who are obviously concerned with communications, do use the British system. Several years ago, a participant at one of my talks woke me up to this fact. When you watch a trial scene in a movie or on TV, watch for the repetition of important testimony. It occurs with great frequency. Recall one of my favorite movies, *My Cousin Vinny*, specifically Joe Pesci's cross-examinations: "*Leaves*, these are *leaves*."

Why would an actor be concerned about reiterating important facts to a jury? The jurors are from central casting and have been paid for their vote. The obvious answer is the actors, or, more to the point, the producers and directors, are not concerned with the jurors, they are concerned with us, the viewing audience. They want to make sure *we* remember what is important. They are professional communicators.

So what can we do to properly and professionally achieve what the British barrister, the old lawyer with supposedly poor hearing, and the actors playing trial lawyers have achieved? We already mentioned one acceptable and very effective communication tool—the blackboard. We can and should simply write on the blackboard important terms or themes used or, in cross-examination, adopted or contributed by the witness.

What else can we do as trial lawyers, now that we better appreciate the need and reason to have a communication device to help jurors remember what is important? Again we go into our trial toolbox, and we now take out the "looping tool." The looping tool is easy to describe, explain, and demonstrate.

Two examples will illustrate how to use the looping tool. Obviously, we wish to repeat the important or operative term or theme. How many times do we want it repeated? The magic number three will usually be the answer. You also will want to consider delayed loops and repetition of the term or theme later in your cross-examination.

Using the Murphy's Bar facts, we will assume the color of the car, green, is the important fact we want the jury to remember. So we will *loop* it.

Q: You saw a car?
A: Yes
Q: A Pontiac?
A: Yes.
Q: Convertible?
A: Yes.
Q: Green?
A: Yes.
Q: You knew the driver of the *green car*?
A: Yes.
Q: Tom Clancy was driving the *green car*?
A: Yes.
Q: The *green car* was going west?
A: Yes.

You have properly repeated or, in the language of trial lawyers, "looped" green car three times. Again, you may wish to do even better by writing "green car" on the blackboard.

What about looping an important theme as distinct from an important term such as green?

Q: It was dark?
A: Yes.
Q: Someone came up behind you *in the dark*?
A: Yes.
Q: Someone took your purse *in the dark*?

A: Yes.
Q: And that someone ran away *in the dark*?
A: Yes.

As suggested, most looping should involve three repetitions. Obviously, this need not always be the case. Later in your cross-examination you may want the important terms and themes repeated still again. But, as is often the circumstance, looping them three more times might be overkill or too much of a good thing. You would then simply loop the important and operative term or theme once. You might consider doing this throughout the cross-examination.

The System, Part II: Statements

8

A. THE THREE WAYS YOU CAN DO CROSS-EXAMINATION

When you hear the statement "Counsel, you may cross-examine," you may, if you elect to cross, proceed in one of three ways. Most probably you will select a combination. The three ways you can cross-examine the witness are:

1. Ask the witness questions, either *regular* or *open-ended.*

Question: Did you go to the store?
Open-ended question: Why did you go to the store?

I do admit, but will never understand why, a very small number of trial lawyers have had success using questions on cross-examination. But for every successful "ask question" cross-examiner, there are 50 lawyers who have done a disservice to their clients by using questions on cross-examination. In truth, this style of cross-examination should have gone out with starched underwear. For that matter, the handful of lawyers who have had success using questions on cross-examination understandably cannot teach others how to do what they do.

Simply stated, cross-examination is not the time for the Discovery Channel, nor is it the time to find out what the case is all about and what the witness knows. "What else do you know about my client, Special Agent Jones?"

Apart from the more obvious problems created by "question" cross-examination, it is defective in that:

a. It invites the witness to participate in the cross-examination. As explained earlier, we do not want the witness to be a cross-examination participant. As a participant, the witness presents in the narrative mode, which enhances his or her credibility. We want witnesses, when we cross-examine them, in the disjunctive[1] mode, which detracts from their credibility.
b. There obviously will be little, if any, control over the witness.
c. You, as the cross-examiner, will have abdicated your valuable right to be the storyteller. Also, the cadence of the story will be interrupted.

2. You may ask the witness traditional leading questions.

Question: You went to the store, isn't that correct?

This form of cross-examination takes much more skill than asking questions, and it is the method probably used by most experienced trial lawyers. It does not invite the witness to participate in the cross-examination, which is a major improvement. It enhances the cross-examiner's control. And it also allows the cross-examiner to become the storyteller, albeit in a somewhat stilted manner.

The problems with the traditional leading question, in ascending order of importance, are:

a. You will never be able to do "one-word cross."
b. You are committing the sin of "legalspeak."You certainly sound like a lawyer, which is not good, when your cross-examination is presented thus:

---

1. Witnesses present in two ways. When in the "disjunctive" mode, their responses are monosyllabic. In the "narrative" mode, they talk and explain.

Q: You went to the store, *isn't that correct*?
Q: You bought some tomatoes, *isn't that correct*?
Q: You bought some potatoes, *isn't that correct*?
Q: You left the store, *isn't that correct*?

c. Finally, and most important, your storytelling leaves much to be desired.

Referring to the illustration above, the repetition of "isn't that correct" or similar leading phrases[2] attenuates your story and is not conducive to proper storytelling.

I came to realize this problem with traditional leading question cross-examination (which at the time was the only known way to properly cross-examine) many years ago. As a young and impressionable faculty member at the National Criminal Defense College, I, along with fortunate others, had the opportunity to sit at the feet of the masters, who regaled us tenderfoots with stories of their trial successes. Almost exclusively the storyteller, being a criminal defense lawyer, related trial successes involving cross-examinations. Interestingly, I noted that their retelling omitted the "traditional leading question" taglines.

They, as was then the practice, used the taglines during the actual trial and when they performed cross-examination demonstrations for the participants. But they omitted them in retelling us what they had done.

Why was this? I certainly did not know the answer then—nor, I suspect, did they. Eventually, several years later, I finally figured it out. To this day I still do not know if they knew why they dropped the taglines in relating their accomplishments; I suspect they did not. I further suspect that they did it instinctively—using their instincts as wonderful storytellers. A proficient storyteller would not tell a story replete with "isn't that correct." They were, each and every one, highly proficient storytellers, so they did not burden their story with these meaningless, unnecessary, and boring terms.

When I finally understood why they were doing what they were

2. "Isn't that right?" Isn't that true?" "Isn't it a fact?" Or even the least offensive, "Right."

doing, I had committed to "storytelling" cross-examination. If the story was better told without the taglines, which was all too obvious, then the taglines had to go.

3. Cross-examine the witness by using *statements*.

Q (using a statement): You went to the store?

Notice the question mark. That is how your statement will appear in a transcript.

How you make the statement is important. Depending upon how you say "you went to the store," it can be heard either as a question or as a definitive statement. You obviously want the latter. This is usually best accomplished by putting the emphasis on the first few and not the ending words.

The advantages of statements over "traditional leading questions," stated in ascending order of importance, are:

a. They make it easier to be short. You will be able to do "one-word cross."
b. They allow you to eliminate the "legalspeak" from your cross-examination.
c. Most important, you will be best positioned to tell your story and to tell it well.

Admittedly, when initially working on this system, I was a bit fearful and apprehensive about the use of statements. Fortunately, my fears and apprehensions were not justified—and for good reason. The use of statements makes sense both legally and practically.

First, the experience of most lawyers who have used and are using the system is that their opponents seldom object, and rarely are such objections sustained. This suggests that trial judges have a great deal of common sense, not to mention a good grasp of the law of evidence. (*See, e.g., Ohio v. Roberts*, 448 U.S. 56, 71 n.11 (1980) (emphasizing that the principal tool and hallmark of cross-examination is the use of leading questions, which counsel phrased as "you never gave . . ."; "this wasn't then in the pack . . ."; and "you never gave them . . .")).

What about an objection by the witness? Unusual, to say the least. But it did happen. Andrea George, an exceptionally able trial lawyer in our Federal Defender office in Minneapolis, Minnesota, shared her experience cross-examining the main prosecution witness in a narcotics trial. Though she won the case, she had two pages of transcript written up to send me.

During Andrea's exceedingly effective cross-examination, the witness suddenly responded to one of her statements by announcing that he objected. The witness complained that she was not asking him questions, and he could only answer "yes" to what she was telling him.

As mentioned, Andrea is an experienced and able trial lawyer. She certainly did not respond to the objection—nor, for that matter, did the judge. Rather, she "tweaked" the witness (explained later) by simply repeating the same statement that had provoked the objection. The witness, his short attempt at being a trial lawyer having ended, dutifully answered "yes."

In summary, you should have no problems using statements as part of the "look good—one-word storytelling" system of cross-examination. This is so because:

a. Seldom will your opponents object, if for no other reason than they do not know what to base their objection on. "Objection, Your Honor. The cross-examiner is destroying my witness" will not be too persuasive.
b. Judges, from the experience of those who use the system, like and welcome this form of cross-examination. Judges are susceptible to being bored, and they are particularly pleased with lawyers who are prepared and move along with purpose. This is especially so on cross-examination. This system forces the lawyer to be totally prepared and, thus, to move along with purpose.
c. Statements are, as a form of leading question, proper on cross-examination.

I have personally used this system before many judges, not only in my own district but from throughout the country. Several years ago I demonstrated the system before the judges of the Seventh Circuit. None of the judges, when critiquing my cross, had any problem with what I was doing. In fact, most commended what I had done.

Over the years, only once was there an objection. It was made not during a trial, but after I had completed a short demonstration on cross-examination. The demonstration took place at an excellent ALI-ABA Trial Evidence in the Federal Courts program ably run by Professor Stephen Saltzburg and an exceptionally bright New York lawyer, Greg Joseph. The objection was made by one of the panelists, an experienced and able trial lawyer. The moderator quite appropriately turned the objection over to the three outstanding federal trial judges who were also on the panel. To a person, they overruled the objection. Instead, all three judges commented favorably on the cross-examination and noted that the witness knew he was being questioned.

Finally, the law supports, albeit not as clearly as I would like, the use of statements as a proper form of leading question (*Ohio v. Roberts*, 448 U.S. 56, 71, 100 S. Ct. 2531, 2541 (1980); *H.L. v. Matheson,* 450 U.S. 398, 401-02, 101 S. Ct. 1164, 1167 (1981)).

Every time I get to thinking that I invented the "statement method" of cross-examination, someone calls my attention to earlier cross-examinations that used statements as a proper form of leading question. As noted, Justice Jackson used statement cross-examination, albeit with little success, in the Nuremberg trials. But history tells us of its proper and successful use as well.

A few years ago, a lawyer from Cleveland, Ohio, Charles E. Evans, having heard me speak on cross-examination, thoughtfully sent me a chapter from a book titled *The Law as Literature*, by Edgar Lustgarten. The chapter most ably covered the trial of Lizzie Borden. The case was tried in New Bedford, Massachusetts, in June of 1893. Both the prosecutor and the defense attorneys proved to be exceptionally able.

The lead defense attorney was George D. Robinson, a former congressman and ex-governor. Some of his cross-examination of the maid Bridget Sullivan is detailed. Note the effective use of statements:

[p. 279] Q: "A pleasant *place* to live?"
A: "Yes sir."
Q: "A pleasant *family* to be in?"
A: "I don't know how the family was . . . I got along alright."

[Author's note: The puppy could have used a "tweaking." This is explained later.]

Q: "You never saw anything *out of the way*?"
A: "No sir."

Q: "Never saw any *quarreling*, or anything of that kind?"
A: "No sir. I did not."
[p. 280] Q: "A pleasant *place* to live?"
A: "Yes."

* * *

[p. 281] Q: "You never saw anything out of the way?"
A: "No sir."
Q: "You never saw any conflict in the family?"
A: "No."
Q: "Never saw any quarreling or anything of that kind?"
A: "No sir."

B. THE LAW

The law is not totally clear about what is and what is not the proper form for cross-examination. The Federal Rules of Evidence and their state counterparts generally permit "leading questions" to be used on cross and instruct courts to exercise reasonable discretion in controlling the order and mode of witness interrogation.[3] Leading questions may be used, but the exact definition of a leading question, and other permissible ways to cross-examine, such as the use of non-leading questions, are not mentioned. There is not much more law than this. Issues concerning the form of questions do not create appellate case law.[4] In other words, the form of cross-examination is a matter for judicial discretion and, indeed, judicial common sense.

The best we can do is define a leading question as one that suggests the answer. A statement would satisfy this definition. A well-written, albeit a dissenting, opinion by Justice LaPrade of the Arizona Supreme Court speaks to this issue and, in effect, concludes that the

---

3. FED. R. EVID. 611 (a) & (c).

4. Most of the scant case law concerns whether leading should be permitted on direct, *see, e.g.,* State v. Hosey, 348 S.E.2d 805, 808 (N.C. 1986), or whether leading should be permitted on cross where the witness is friendly although not technically adverse. *Also see, e.g.,* Schultz v. Rice, 809 F.2d 643, 654 (10th Cir. 1986). Case law does not define "leading question" beyond the textbook definition of "[a question] that suggests to the witness the answer desired by the examiner." MCCORMICK ON EVIDENCE § 6 (4th ed. 1992).

traditional leading question and a statement are essentially the same. (*State v. Scofield*, 7 Ariz. App. 307, 438 P.2d 776 (1968).)

Unfortunately, the case facts are a bit convoluted. On direct examination of a child witness, the prosecutor used both traditional leading questions and statements. Justice LaPrade criticized the use of leading questions, both the traditional leading questions and the statements, both of which he referred to as "leading questions." He thought they were inappropriate during *direct* examination.

The use of short statements during cross-examination sounds good, moves along well, and judges like this system. In truth and in logic, a statement is a proper leading question. It, as the traditional leading question, suggests the answer, but obviously it does so without the cumbersome legalese. As we have seen, this system makes for a quick pace and demands concise language anyone can understand. Nobody likes long, boring lawyerisms. Short, crisp statements have the sound of moving things along. If you tell someone about a conversation you had, you say, "I asked him if he saw a car." You never say, "I asked him if it was correct to say that he saw a car." Judges will like this, jurors prefer it, and it just plain makes sense.

As a practical matter, you will seldom receive an objection to using the system. But what if you do get an objection? The occasional and unusual objection will come in the form of "Your Honor, I object. This is improper cross," or the slightly more sophisticated "Your Honor, I object. Counsel is not asking questions." (As mentioned earlier, cross-examination is not the time to be asking questions.)

Your response is important. Here is another MacCarthyism on trial advocacy, one not limited to this situation. You have just had an evidence objection, and obviously you want the judge to rule for you. Step one: Look at the judge. Step two: Use your head. (Recall Rule 37, the head nod.) You are ready for step three. With your head nodding up and down, say, "As Your Honor well knows . . . ." Always use that phrase, followed by a reference to the law—preferably a legal citation.

Attorney: As Your Honor well knows, the United States Supreme Court in *Ohio v. Roberts* said this is not the only proper but the only way for a lawyer to cross-examine [with the head nodding].

As mentioned earlier, if you nod your head up and down, the judge's head will nod up and down as well. With his head nodding up and down, a judge will not say the word "no." If you try to say "no" with your head moving up and down, you will probably hurt yourself. OK, this is not foolproof, but it usually works well.

By using the phrase "As Your Honor well knows . . . ," you have accorded infinite knowledge and wisdom to the judge. This impresses clerks, bailiffs, marshals, jurors, and, most of all, judges. Her Honor knows this; she knows the law. She will not want to destroy that effect or reject the compliment. So her head will also go up and down. She will probably rule for you.

There are two problems with the above suggestion. The more serious problem is that *Ohio v. Roberts*, 448 U.S. 56 (1980), does not exactly say that lawyers are permitted to use statements on cross-examination. Nevertheless, *Ohio v. Roberts* is a case about cross-examination. The Supreme Court gives examples of good cross-examination, calling it "cross-examination as a matter of form." *Roberts*, 448 U.S. at 71 n.11. Four of the seven examples cited are statements.[5] *Id.*

The second problem, a more recent concern, is that Justice Scalia's exceptionally able opinion in *Crawford v. Washington*, 541 U.S. 36 (2004), overrules *Ohio v. Roberts*, 448 U.S. 56 (1980). Though *Crawford* overrules *Ohio v. Roberts*, Crawford does not address or overrule the comments of the Court on what constitutes proper cross-examination.

Another Supreme Court case that can be cited as support for the use of statements is *H.L. v. Matheson*, 450 U.S. 398, 101 S. Ct. 1164 (1981). Admittedly, the case is not about cross-examination. It is a civil case, but actually it is an even better case about statements being a proper form of leading question. A transcript of the examination of a witness appears in footnote 6, p. 401. All 16 questions listed are statements to which the witness gave, as our system suggests, one-word affirmative responses. The main opinion and the concurrence both comment on the fact that "leading questions" were used in examining

5. No less than 17 plainly leading questions were asked, as indicated by phrases in counsel's inquiries: "is[n't] it a fact . . . that"; "is it to your knowledge, then, that . . ."; "is[n't] that correct"; "you never gave them . . ."; "this wasn't then in the pack . . ."; "you have never [not] seen [discussed, talked] . . ."; "you never gave . . . ."

the witness. Again, these "leading questions" were all statements. Unfortunately and embarrassingly, the examination referred to was a direct examination. The cross-examination, also quoted from, was done in a form we are trying to eliminate.

Even without supporting case law, judges are likely to accept this system because it concerns cross-examination. I speak now as a criminal defense lawyer and my biases are obvious, but when I started practicing law some years ago, they gave us a big trial advocacy toolbox full of tools for criminal defense. Sadly, today we have the same box but far fewer tools. Over the years, judges, prosecutors and, in particular, legislators have conspired to take many of these tools from us. Voir dire is almost gone. The Fourth Amendment is not what it used to be. Historically, when we win a case, whatever tool we use to win is taken from us.

Only one tool has remained sacred, and that is the right to cross-examine witnesses.[6] Judges are, with good reason, hesitant to get into areas where they limit cross-examination. They may limit, as well they should, repetitive or irrelevant cross-examination, but not cross-examination itself. For this reason alone, judges will not prohibit you from using this system of cross-examination.

Statements are a proper form of leading question, and you have a right to use them. There is nothing wrong with it. I have used this system before many of the best judges in the country and they love it, they think it is wonderful, and there is nothing proscribing it. From a communications standpoint, it makes sense to use short, clear statements. Lawyerisms such as "isn't it a fact that" are pure formalism; there is no reason why they should not go the way of the powdered wig.

Finally, anticipating the worst, here is what to do if an objection to your style of cross is sustained.

Attorney: You saw a car.
Opponent: Your Honor, I object. This is improper cross-examination. She's not asking questions.

---

6. *See, e.g.,* Davis v. Alaska, 415 U.S. 308 (1974) (conviction reversed where defendant was prohibited from cross-examining government witness about juvenile convictions for which witness was still on probation); Olden v. Kentucky, 488 U.S. 227 (1988) (conviction reversed for undue restriction of cross-examination).

The Court: Sustained. Ask questions.
Attorney: You saw a car [looking at opponent], *right*?
Witness: Yes.
Attorney: Going west [looking at opponent], *right*?
Witness: Yes.
Attorney: You knew the driver [looking at opponent], *right*?
Witness: Yes.
Attorney: Tom Clancy was driving [looking at opponent], *right*?
Witness: Yes.
Attorney: There was a woman in the car.

This last time you skipped the word "right." At this point, the happiest person in the courtroom is your idiot opponent who brought this all about with his stupid objection. He is thankful to be off the hook. The judge is also pleased that we have stopped playing "Simon Says." And finally, the jurors are delighted that you will be able to go uninterrupted back to talking like a human being and not a game participant.

C. THE SYSTEM HAS A PHILOSOPHY

Now that we have settled on statements, how about this: "You went to the store to buy toothpaste and magazines?" You are initially tempted to say "this is fine, it is a statement." But then you realize that, though it is a statement, it violates our requirement to be short. It is much too long to satisfy the system.

Actually, every person who uses the system gets a report card. Looking at that report card, I can tell you how well or how poorly you did your cross-examination.

The report card is a simple one, not unlike the one you received in the first and second grades. You get stars, gold, silver or bronze, depending on the degree of your accomplishment. Every time the witness answers "yes," you get a gold star. Every time the witness answers "no," and "no" was the desired answer, you get a silver star. Every time the witness answers "I don't know" or "I don't remember," you get a bronze star. At the end of the cross-examinations, the best cross-examination is the one with the most stars, preferably gold. If the result is anything but a star, you get either an "incomplete" or a negative mark.

Let us return to: "You went to the store to buy toothpaste and magazines?" Though it is a statement, you would only get one gold star. You want and need as many as you can get consistent with not being repetitious or boring the jury. To demonstrate, albeit with a boring, shaggy dog story:

Q: I want to ask you some questions about what you did when you got ready to go to the store, you understand?
A: Yes.
Q: You left your apartment?
A: Yes.
Q: You walked over to your car?
A: Yes.
Q: It was parked on the street?
A: Yes.
Q: You got in the car?
A: Yes.
Q: You started the motor?
A: Yes.
Q: You drove away?
A: Yes.
Q: You drove to the store?
A: Yes.
Q: The grocery store?
A: Yes.
Q: The Jewel store?
A: Yes.
Q: You parked your car?
A: Yes.
Q: In the store parking lot?
A: Yes.
Q: You went in the store?
A: Yes.
Q: I want to ask you some questions about what you did in the store, you understand?
A: Yes.
Q: You went to the toothpaste counter?
A: Yes.
Q: Picked up a tube of toothpaste?

A: Yes.
Q: Then you went to the magazine counter?
A: Yes.
Q: You looked at the magazines?
A: Yes.
Q: You picked up two magazines?
A: Yes.
Q: You then went to the checkout counter?
A: Yes.
Q: You talked to the lady behind the counter?
A: Yes.
Q: And she talked to you?
A: Yes.
Q: You paid for the toothpaste?
A: Yes.
Q: You paid for the magazines?
A: Yes.
Q: Both magazines?
A: Yes.
Q: Then you left the store?
A: Yes.

And of course, if you want, you can go on with this boring, no-punch-line story. We shall not. The point I am making is that this cross would get me an excellent report card. I had 26 gold stars.

Enough boredom, let's make the point. Again, the more stars, preferably gold, the better. Why? For three reasons.

1. In cross-examination, it is your job to train the puppy (the witness). You are doing an excellent job of this. You will have put the puppy (witness) into the "yes mode." Soon the puppy will stop thinking about content and, satisfied that you know everything and that this cross-examination is not all that bad, will lock into the "yes" mode. All he has to do is simply answer "yes," and everything goes smoothly.
2. If everything you say is answered "yes," your credibility, of critical importance, will be greatly enhanced. Actually, this is

of even greater importance than training the puppy. You will have attained "ethical appeal" where the speaker and the speech become more credible.

3. Finally, you will be telling a story—hopefully, one considerably better than the one I just told.

Having explained the system's philosophy and purpose, this is the time to consider what many friends, good trial lawyers all, have suggested. "Why not, when you know the answer, simply ask the witness a question?" They believe this would be a "good change of pace." They believe this would make us look less dominating.

Indeed, it would be a change of pace. And we would appear less dominating. However, for these minor accomplishments we would pay a large price.

The doctor you are cross-examining took a blood-alcohol reading from Mr. O'Brien. The reading result was .025. O'Brien was legally drunk, or, if you prefer, intoxicated. Following the system, the cross-examination would simply go as follows:

Q: I want to ask you some questions about the blood-alcohol test you did on Mr. O'Brien.
A: Yes.
Q: That test gave you a reading?
A: Yes.
Q: That reading was .025?
A: Yes.
Q: Mr. O'Brien was legally drunk?
A: Yes.

A few friends, seeking to be helpful, would suggest this change.

Q: That test gave you a reading?
A: Yes.
Q: WHAT WAS THAT READING?

At first glance, this use of a question does not seem unreasonable. It invites the witness to think and explain. However, you are all too aware of Murphy's Law: "If anything can go wrong, it will."

A: Well, the reading was .025, but that number can be misleading. First off, this was taken three hours after the fight. The reading would have much lower then. Also, Mr. O'Brien is an exceptionally big man. He weighs almost 300 pounds. A 150-pound man would probably be drunk with a .025 reading, but a man twice that size may not have been drunk.

Murphy's Law does happen! Then again, even if it does not happen, you still lose. Now go back to the system's philosophy and purpose.

1. You have worked hard to get the puppy trained, to get the puppy into the "yes" mode. This one question destroys your accomplishments. Suddenly you have taken the puppy off the leash and allowed, indeed encouraged, it to tinkle.
2. The credibility points are now given to the witness and not to you. By asking the question of the witness, you exacerbate the problem in that you are, in effect, sponsoring the witness. You are accrediting your opponent's witness. And, of course, you lose the credibility points.
3. You have abdicated your role and your right to be the storyteller. You have made the witness the storyteller. Consequently, he will be presenting in the narrative form, enhancing rather than diminishing his credibility.

Do not be tempted to take the easy path and ask questions.

D. CRAFTING YOUR STATEMENTS

In crafting our statements, there are several things we should keep in mind. Most of these are obvious, though some are often forgotten.

- Leave extraneous details out of your statements. These details often allow and encourage the witness to either deny the statement or offer some sort of narrative response. If the extraneous detail is important to you, then make it a statement unto itself.
- Your statements should state facts and not opinions.
- Where possible, frame your statements in a positive rather than a negative manner. Positive statements are easier to understand

and will lead to preferable "yes" answers. "No" answers, though sometimes necessary as a better fit with our story line, are good, but they are not as good as "yes" answers.

- When drawing the "no" response, it is best to run a short series of them.

Q: I want to ask you some questions about your investigation.
A: Yes.
Q: You told us what you saw?
A: Yes.
Q: And you told us what you did?
A: Yes.
Q: You never mentioned John Jones's name?
A: No.
Q: John Jones was not at the car wash?
A: No.
Q: You did not meet with John Jones at Denny's?
A: No.
Q: John Jones did not hand you any cocaine?
A: No.
Q: And you did not hand John Jones any money?
A: No.
Q: While you were making this deal, no one ever mentioned John Jones's name?
A: No.

Notice that the last six questions asked for (and received) "no" answers. By grouping negatively phrased questions together, you reap most of the same advantages as you would by asking positive questions. The witness becomes trained to give a repetitive one-word answer.

Historically, one of the best examples of putting the witness in the "no" mode was Clarence Darrow's cross-examination of Police Inspector Norton Schuknecht in the Detroit *Sweet* trial. Partway through his cross-examination, Darrow shifted into a series of questions (yes, he asked questions, but then again, he *was* Clarence Darrow) to discredit Schuknecht by showing that he, Schuknecht, did not do a series of things that a good and competent police officer would have done. It was, to say the least, effective. (See Kevin Boyle, *Arc of Justice*, p. 274.)

A few examples of negative and positive phrasing follow.

Negative Phrasing	Positive Phrasing
You do not drink your coffee black?	You drink coffee? With cream? With sugar? Not black?
You had not met John Jones before?	That was the first time you met John Jones?

- Avoid conclusive statements. These invite unwanted witness participation. A helpful reminder is, in most instances, to avoid beginning a statement with "yet," "still," "so," or "therefore." These introductory words usually signal a conclusion or possibly a contradiction.
- Avoid arguments. Statements containing values and judgements are likely to prompt argument. In *Trying Cases to Win*, Herbert Stern dissects Justice Jackson's attempted cross-examination of Hermann Goering at Nuremberg. Instead of confronting Goering with facts and dates, Jackson asked Goering incomprehensibly long questions loaded with values, judgments, and philosophy. Naturally, he received long answers disputing the assumptions of the questions. This is a sure formula for losing control. If you find yourself arguing with a witness, retreat to facts. Paint a clear picture with the facts, and the jury will take care of the values and judgments.

Commenting on the cross-examination in the Nuremberg trials, I suggest that the British prosecutor, a Mr. G. D. Roberts, was far and away the best cross-examiner. He commendably made use of traditional leading questions, usually using the suffix "that is right" or "is that right." That said, he would have been much better had he read and employed the teaching of this book.

The Russian prosecutors had the right idea. They simply told the witnesses what they, the prosecutors, wanted to hear. Unfortunately, they did so in a most inelegant manner, totally inconsistent with good and proper trial advocacy. The witnesses, obviously, did not agree with them.

As mentioned, Justice Jackson, the American prosecutor, demonstrated his long absence from the trial bar. Commendably, he often used statements; unfortunately, they were anything but short statements. He also availed himself of open-ended questions. The result, in particular with Hermann Goering on the stand, was dialogue cross-examination. Both the lawyer and the witness spoke at length. The witness had to and did win, given the format.

E. DETAILS

A famous Chinese philosopher or general said that all battles are won or lost before they are actually fought. Similarly, President Dwight Eisenhower, speaking as a general, said, "In preparing for battle I have always found that plans are useless, but planning is indispensable."

And, finally, one of my favorites: Muhammad Ali observed, "The fight is won or lost far away from witnesses—before the lines, in the gym and out there on the road, long before I dance under these lights."

Accepting these suggestions, you must know your facts, and they must be accurate—they will be the facts you will use to tell your story.

Exact details and sources of information

We have talked about various techniques used to get the witness to answer "yes." Admittedly, there are a few excellent trial lawyers who are not particularly concerned with the witness's response. Their emphasis is on what they are telling the jurors. This makes some sense, but I am obviously also concerned with the witness's response and not merely what I, the cross-examiner, am saying. The most obvious requirement, then, is that you make statements that the witness will agree with.

For many years I and, I suspect, most criminal defense lawyers crossed on the basis of what the witness said on direct examination. The notes we took during the direct were the source of material upon which we would cross. We had a general idea about the issues we would like to see developed. And, of course, we had a good idea of material we could use to impeach the witness. Still, what the witness said on direct served to give us our material for cross-examination.

This was a terrible way to go about cross-examination. You may well get or benefit from something the witness says on direct. Consider that a bonus and concern yourself with where, in your storyline, you want to develop this bonus material.

Before the witness ever speaks a word on direct, you must have your cross-examination completely outlined. You must have your story ready to tell, with short statements. Wanting, as we do, for the witness to agree with us, we must use only accurate facts and details, to which the witness must respond "yes."

F. TERMS

As a trial lawyer, you have a responsibility to select and use the terms, words, and expressions that best serve the story you want to tell.

When preparing your case for trial, you must make a list of the "good facts" and the "bad facts." List the terms you want used and those you do not want used. If you have a proper legal reason to keep certain terms out, file a motion *in limine*.

Following are a few reminders about your use of terms.

1. No Legalese

As much as I enjoyed law school (I know and appreciate that many of you did not), it left me with baggage in my quest to be a trial lawyer. In law school we were taught and expected to talk like lawyers. Our professors and fellow students talked like lawyers. In the law school classroom, this was not a liability. However, those of us who sought to become trial lawyers had problems, which were exacerbated by our working with other trial lawyers—particularly prosecutors.

"Did you go to the store?" became "Did there come a time when you went to the store?" We also liked and used "Did you have occasion to . . . ?" "Where, if anywhere, did you go?" "Did you see a man who you later knew to be Mr. Cobb?" This "legalese" violated my Trial Advocacy Rule 11: "You speak in a courtroom the way you speak in a bar."

The very best criticism of legalese can be found in the brilliant opinion of Judge Duniway in *United States v. Marshall*, 488 F.2d 1169 (9th Cir. 1973). Admittedly, the judge was talking about federal agents, but, as we all know, prosecutors, criminal defense attorneys, and civil trial lawyers are inclined to adopt the language of the agents.

In *Marshall,* Judge Duniway wrote a lengthy footnote—actually, three consecutive footnotes—that carried over several pages of the opinion (*id.* at 1171 n.1-2, 1176 n.3). I enjoy using a few lines of his footnote when teaching trial advocacy and a participant starts using legalese. I sentence them to read out loud a portion of the judge's footnote.

Though I am not one to quote extensively from judicial opinions, this is an exception:

> The agents involved speak an almost impenetrable jargon. They do not get into their cars; they enter official government vehicles. They do not get out of or leave their cars, they exit them. They do not go somewhere; they proceed. They do not go to a particular place; they proceed to its vicinity. They do not watch or look; they surveille [sic]. They never see anything; they observe it. No one tells them anything; they are advised. A person does not tell them his name; he identifies himself. A person does not say something; he indicates. They do not listen to a telephone conversation; they monitor it. People telephoning to each other do not say "hello"; they exchange greetings. An agent does not hand money to an informer to make a buy; he advances previously recorded official government funds. To an agent, a list of serial numbers does not list serial numbers, it depicts Federal Reserve Notes. An agent does not say what an exhibit is; he says that it purports to be. The agents preface answers to simple and direct questions with "to my knowledge." They cannot describe a conversation by saying "he said" and "I said"; they speak in conclusions. Sometimes it takes the combined efforts of counsel and the judge to get them to state who said what. Under cross-examination, they seem unable to give a direct answer to a question; they either spout conclusions or do not understand. This often gives the prosecutor, under the guise of an objection, an opportunity to suggest an answer, which is then obligingly given.

Marshall, 488 F.2d at 1171 n.1.

Throughout this opinion, we quote the reporter's transcript line for line, with all indentations, for reasons that will later appear. (This statement does not apply to transcript quotations in the footnotes.) Much of what we say is supported by the portions of the transcript that are later quoted in this opinion. We add here a few items from the testimony of agent Hoelker:

> Q: Well, did you go there to go in and search the house and search the people?
> Q: Mr. Hoelker, you use these words "official advance funds." Actually, this was money wasn't it?
> A: That is correct.
> Q: Just like any other money?
> A: No, sir, it is not like just any other money.
> *Witness:* Are you asking me if I went to the cash register [in a store] and identified that bill and that serial number?
> A: Yes. I would retrieve it as evidence, yes, I would, and I could.
> Q: And would you demand that that—whoever the storekeeper was, identify themselves to you?
> A: That is correct.

Marshall, id. at n.2

Remember that the events described occurred in a private home, which the agents had entered without a warrant and without the consent of the occupants, as we show hereafter.

The agents' definition of the phrase "secure a residence" is both fascinating and disturbing. Alden testified at some length on the subject.

> Q: And what do you mean by secure? Would you distinguish it from search?
> A: Yes.
> Q: Would you tell the court what the difference is?
> A: To enter a residence and make sure—gather the people, get them together and make sure that—how do I explain it? I can explain search better. Search would be to physically go through the house and go through each of the rooms, the closets, the cupboards—everything like that. To secure is to bring under control.
> Q: Did you ever give directions that the house be searched?
> A: No.

. . . .

When you secure a residence you have to make sure that you—you have to check all of the rooms to make sure there is no one hiding, you know, hiding in a closet with a gun at your back, so you have to secure the whole residence and search individuals for weapons. You cannot just go in one room and there are ten people in the other room. You have to secure the whole residence.

. . . .

Q: Explain it to us, please, what did you mean by securing the residence?
A: To take control of it.
Q: And what do you mean by taking control of, then?
A: Take control of.
Q: Well, to take control of—but what did you mean for those men to do?
A: To take physical control of the residence.
Q: Outside and inside?
A: Yes—well, not outside, not the street, no.
Q: Well, as far as that house was concerned, then, you directed your men to go take control of the inside of that residence, did you not?
A: Yes.
Q: And by taking control of the inside of the residence, what did you intend for your agents to do?
A: What did I intend them to do?
Q: In other words, when you said to take control of the inside of that residence, what was your intent that they do?
A: Take control of it.
Q: By that, did you mean that they were to go there and, with or without the consent of the people there, go into the house and go into each room and look and see what they might see?
A: I didn't quite understand all of that. . . . I instructed them to secure the residence—take control, to enter the residence—to take control of the residence. Whatever was necessary to take control of the residence.

. . . .

Q: That means to go and to go into each room and look?
A: For their safety, yes.
Q: What do these things you are talking about, "their safety," you mean for them to do or not to do?

A: Do what?
Q: To go in there and look in each room and see what they can see.
A: Yes, that is part of the procedure when you take control.
Q: And did you intend for them to go in there and search it?
A: Frisk.
Q: Frisk each person in the house?
A: Frisk.

. . . .

Agent Willis's testimony is similar.

Q: What do you mean by "secure"? What is the different [sic] between secure and search?
A: There is a difference, sir.
Q: All right. Now tell us about it. You went there and you went with your guns and badges and you went in and searched all of the people and you went into all of the rooms and the closet, didn't you?
A: No, sir.
Q: You didn't?
A: No, sir.
Q: I asked you if you didn't sign an affidavit before you came here to the court with regard to this case.
A: An affidavit was prepared and I did sign one.
Q: All right. The last sentence of that affidavit is, as I read it, that each room and closet was looked into to insure that no possible armed subjects remained at large. Now, did you look into each closet in each room or not?
A: We looked into the closets. We didn't search the closets.

Marshall, *id.* at 1176 n.3.

Having read the above, you should be cured of the legalese trap.

2. Use Power Language

Actually, this suggestion is best stated in the negative. You want to avoid hedges, fillers, deferential expressions, and intensifiers.[7] Get rid

7. *See* WILLIAM M. O'BARR, LINGUISTIC EVIDENCE: LANGUAGE, POWER, AND STRAGEGY IN THE COURTROOM (Academic Press 1982).

of the "maybe," "possibly," "probably," "I think," and "I believe." Also avoid "so," "very," and "really."

Though it can prove a difficult thing to do once you have fallen into the habit, you must work on eliminating verbal ticks. Many of us repeat these terms, which distract from rather than aid our storytelling. We must then work on eliminating unnecessary beginnings to our statements: "and," "okay" (one that I have suffered with), "like," and "well."

3. Carefully Select and Use Your Terms

Trial lawyers brainstorm their cases. Again, the theory of the case is usually obvious. The themes of the case, both good and bad, are the raw material from which your trial story is created.

In addition to listing the good and bad themes, you must also list the good and the bad terms. This takes a bit of skill and some experience. If you are defending a case involving two cars going in different directions, you will refer to the "accident." Your opponent will call it a "collision," or even a "terrible collision." These terms, which create totally different pictures, are important.

I vividly remember the Hoftus and Palmer 1974 research study. The experiment involved a car accident and some of the terms used to describe it. Several groups of people were simultaneously shown a film of the car accident. All saw exactly the same scene.

The groups were then asked to write down about how fast the cars were going when they "hit" each other. The adjectives used with the groups varied in intensity. As the adjectives got more severe, so did the participants' judgment of the speed of the cars.

Judicial approbation for the use of your terms is found in the Seventh Circuit opinion in *United States v. Levine*, 180 F.3d 868 (7th Cir. 1999). Not surprisingly, in that the opinion is pro-cross, the court was commenting on the prosecutor's cross-examination. The prosecutor asked the defendant whether he "forged" signatures. The defense objected that this called for a legal conclusion. The court properly concluded that the real objection was the prosecutor's use of "a word freighted with connotations of wrongdoing." That said, the court concluded:

> [P]utting one's own spin on events is a principal use of cross-examination. Witnesses can't insist that the prosecutor use euphemisms. . . .

Id.

> The difference between the almost right word and the right word is really a large matter—'tis the difference between the lightning bug and the lightning.
>
> Mark Twain in George Bainton,
> *The Art of Authorship* (1890), pp. 87-88.

G. ORGANIZATION—SOURCE OF MATERIALS

There are three sources of material you can use to cross-examine: witness statements, verisimilitude, and plausibility.

1. Witness Statements

There have been times, while working with a group, when I have been asked to or wanted to demonstrate the system. The problem was I did not know the facts in the case. I could still do a demonstration[8] of the system, even though I was not, as one must do in a real trial, using a story to develop a case theme. I simply picked up the witness statement and, reading from it, I would use short statements while trying to maintain some order and coherence.

The point I make is that the witness statement has much material from which you can prepare your cross-examination statements. Unlike my demonstration, you will be prepared, you will know your facts and your issues, and you will use the witness statement to develop your story line.

As a criminal defense lawyer, I obviously need more than witness statements, which often do not exist or materialize late in the game. There are then two other sources of material to help us in preparing our cross-examination statements.

2. Verisimilitude

The second source is what I call verisimilitude material. The way things were or are: the truth. This source lends itself to some interesting teach-

---

8. Recall the motto of the criminal defense lawyer: "Always ready, seldom prepared." (Thank you, Dale Cobb.)

ing demonstrations. Once again, the demonstration is limited in that we will not be developing a theme, but we can and will demonstrate the use of verisimilitude in the system.

Either from those working the seminar registration table or from talking to a particular participant, I can obtain some basic information about my eventual witnesses. That limited information is my segue into verisimilitude cross-examination.[9]

Attorney: I want to ask you some questions about what you did when you got up this morning, you understand?
Witness: Yes.
Attorney: You got dressed?
Witness: Yes.
Attorney: You put on a shirt?
Witness: Yes.
Attorney: A white shirt?
Witness: Yes.
Attorney: A white golf shirt?
Witness: Yes.
Attorney: There was writing over the left pocket?
Witness: Yes.
Attorney: The writing was in blue?
Witness: Yes.
Attorney: It said Brown's Lake Golf Course?
Witness: Yes.
Attorney: You put on trousers?[10]
Witness: Yes.
Attorney: Blue trousers?
Witness: Yes.
Attorney: You wore a belt?
Witness: Yes.
Attorney: A black belt?
Witness: Yes.
Attorney: You put on socks?

9. This cross-examination is also helpful in showing a "doubting Thomas" how difficult it is to be an intractable witness.

10. OK, most people would use the term "pants." However, having served in the United States Marine Corps, this is the term I use.

Witness: Yes.
Attorney: Blue socks?
Witness: Yes.
Attorney: And shoes?
Witness: Yes.
Attorney: Black shoes?
Witness: Yes.
Attorney: Loafers?
Witness: Yes.

Note: All of this verisimilitude information comes from looking at the witness.[11]

Attorney: Now I want to ask you what you did when you left your house, your understand?
Witness: Yes.
Attorney: You got in your car?
Witness: Yes.
Attorney: You started to drive away?
Witness: Yes.
Attorney: To downtown Chicago?
Witness: Yes.
Attorney: You were alone?
Witness: Yes.
Attorney: No friends? (This is put in for some humor in what could otherwise be a boring demonstration.)
Witness: Right.
Attorney: You drove to the Palmer House Hotel?
Witness: Yes.
Attorney: You gave your car to the valet?

---

11. Some years ago, Professor Deryl Dantzler, the dean of the National Criminal Defense College, prepared an incredible piece on cross-examination. It influenced my thinking on cross-examination and, eventually, my system more than anything else I had read. She called her work *Why Johnny Can't Lead*. Her particularly effective drill had participants cross-examine on what another person was wearing. This was all verisimilitude cross-examination. It was also a wonderful way to learn how to control a witness. *See Cross-Examination,* in DEAN DERYL D. DANTZLER, WHY JOHNNY CAN'T LEAD AND SOME OTHER OBSERVATIONS (National Criminal Defense College).

Witness: Yes.
Attorney: You went into the hotel?
Witness: Yes.
Attorney: To the seventh floor?
Witness: Yes.
Attorney: The Blue Room?
Witness: Yes.
Attorney: There were two ladies in the hallway?
Witness: Yes.
Attorney: You knew what they were doing?
Witness: Yes.
Attorney: They were registering those attending the seminar?
Witness: Yes.
Attorney: You talked to them?
Witness: Yes.
Attorney: They talked to you? (another MacCarthyism)
Witness: Yes.
Attorney: They gave you some material?
Witness: Yes.
Attorney: An outline?
Witness: Yes.
Attorney: An outline entitled "Look Good Cross"?
Witness: Yes.
Attorney: Now I want to ask you what you did after you received your outline, you understand?
Witness: Yes.
Attorney: You went into the Blue Room?
Witness: Yes.
Attorney: You saw some people you knew?
Witness: Yes.
Attorney: You also saw some people you did not know?
Witness: Yes.
Attorney: You found a place to sit down?
Witness: Yes.
Attorney: You sat next to a friend?
Witness: Yes.
Attorney: Your friend's name was Steve Shanin?
Witness: Yes.

Attorney: I want to ask you some questions about the Blue Room, you understand?
Witness: Yes.
Attorney: There were tables in the room?
Witness: Yes.
Attorney: The tables faced the lectern?
Witness: Yes.
Attorney: There were chairs?
Witness: Yes.
Attorney: There were water pitchers on the tables?
Witness: Yes.
Attorney: There were glasses on the tables?
Witness: Yes.
Attorney: Much of the room was painted blue?
Witness: Yes.
Attorney: There were wall hangings on the back wall?
Witness: Yes.

In truth, there were no wall hangings on the back wall. However, if the witness is in the "yes" mode, inevitably he or she will simply answer "yes." I do not suggest you cross with this type of story line. Still, you can and should use some of this filler to get the witness in the "yes" mode.

Actually, verisimilitude covers much more. It also covers impactive material not found in the witness statement. What is the truth, what are the facts, what were things like?

I immediately think of potential impeachment. The witness is a convicted felon, he is a liar, he has a reason to twist the truth. All of these things and much more can be used under the verisimilitude heading.

3. Plausibility

The final source of cross-examination material is a very special and powerful one, plausibility cross-examination. Verisimilitude is the way things were or are; plausibility is the way the jury thinks they were or are. Usually these will be the same.

Early on, I used plausibility cross when demonstrating the basic system using the Murphy's Bar example. After our story had taken the witness out of the bar, recall the statement "you looked around." Most probably the fact that the witness "looked around" is not in this statement. This is something not normally included in a statement because it is not of particular importance. Still we want to use it, because it is part of our story line. We also want to use it because it is a plausibility statement, albeit not a particularly significant one. The plausibility statement gives the witness the option either of simply answering "yes," which we can and will accept, or of fighting you. Truth be known, you will gain more if the witness fights you.

Someone coming out of any place, no less a bar, looks around. The jury will not believe that someone coming out of Murphy's Bar would cover their eyes so as not to look around. Besides, the witness will, later in the cross, detail what he saw. To see these things, he had to look around.

There are many other examples of plausibility cross-examination far more impactive than "you looked around." The following should be used when cross-examining a snitch or cooperating witness: "You do not want to go to jail?" "You would like to avoid going to jail?" "You would do most anything to avoid going to jail?"

In a civil case: "You do not want your employer to lose this case?" "You want to make money off of this case?" "Making money is important to you?" "You would do most anything to make a large sum of money?"

Some of you may remember the hearings to confirm then-Judge Clarence Thomas to be an Associate Justice of the United States Supreme Court. During the hearings, one of the senators asked the judge whether he had ever discussed *Roe v. Wade*, 410 U.S. 113 (1973), with anybody. Though I am not sure whether the senator had intended it as such, this was excellent plausibility, though expressed as a question rather than a statement. What information did we have that might bear on the Justice's response?

Justice Thomas went to Yale Law School. He was in law school in 1973 when the United States Supreme Court decided *Roe v. Wade*, which is one of the most significant political cases in recent history. When extremely important cases come out of the United States Supreme Court while you are in law school, you talk about them. That is what law school is all about; professors and law school students talk about these critically important cases.

After law school, Justice Thomas went on to become a mover and shaker in one of the major political parties. And now, appreciating that background, he was asked if he ever talked about *Roe v. Wade* with anybody. What could he answer? He could have answered "yes," which for whatever reason he apparently did not want to do. Instead, he chose to answer "no." It does not matter whether Justice Thomas was telling the truth or not; he was given a choice between saying "yes" or giving an answer that was completely implausible, though possibly truthful.

Lest I be accused of being politically motivated, I offer not a statement but a response, which, though again possibly true, lacked plausibility: "Yes, I smoked marijuana but I did not inhale."[12]

These responses are on a par with "the dog ate my homework." As a cross-examiner, you want to invite and encourage the witness to respond in an implausible fashion.

To incorporate some of these diverse suggestions, let us consider a typical criminal case. The principal witness against your Johnny is the cellmate who says, "In the five minutes I knew Johnny, he confessed a bank robbery to me. Now, can I get a break on my car theft rap?"

From his statement, you know that the snitch was home on January 1, 2005, watching football on television, by himself. There was a knock at the door, and before he could answer it, the door was knocked down. Two police officers came in and arrested him for car theft. He was put in jail. About a month later, they put your client, Johnny, in jail with him. Twenty-four hours later, the snitch swears that Johnny confessed to robbing the First National Bank.

Attorney: Now, I am going to ask you some questions about what happened when you were arrested on January 1, you understand?
Witness: OK.
Attorney: You were in your apartment?
Witness: Yes.
Attorney: Watching TV?

12. I understand and appreciate President Clinton's autobiographical attempts to explain that he did not smoke, and for that reason he could not inhale. I would believe this, but I doubt most others would.

Witness: Yes.
Attorney: Watching football?
Witness: Yes.
Attorney: You were alone?
Witness: Yes.
Attorney: No friends? (Yes, I like this one.)
Witness: Right.
Attorney: There was a knock at your door?
Witness: Yes.

You should knock on the lectern at this point; it will add to your storytelling.

Attorney: You got up from where you were sitting?
Witness: Yes.
Attorney: But not fast enough?
Witness: Yes.
Attorney: As a matter of fact, the door came flying in?
Witness: Yes.
Attorney: Splinters all over the room? [verisimilitude]
Witness: Yes.
Attorney: Two men came in?
Witness: Yes.
Attorney: They looked at you? [verisimilitude]
Witness: Yes.
Attorney: You looked at them? [verisimilitude]
Witness: Yes.
Attorney: They had guns in their hands?

Let the jury see the guns by holding up your right index finger in the form of a gun.

Witness: Yes.
Attorney: They pointed those guns at you?
Witness: Yes.
Attorney: You were concerned?
Witness: Yes.
Attorney: You were afraid?
Witness: Yes.

Attorney: You were scared?
Witness: Yes.

Now, by the way, "scared" is not in the witness's statement. It does not matter. You know he was scared. What can he say, "no?" That is a plausibility statement. Also note the trilogy: concerned, afraid, and scared.

Attorney: They ran up to you?
Witness: Yes.
Attorney: They told you to put your hands behind your back?
Witness: Yes.
Attorney: You put your hands behind your back?
Witness: Yes.
Attorney: They put a handcuff on your right wrist?
Witness: Yes.
Attorney: They handcuffed it to your left wrist?
Witness: Yes.
Attorney: Behind your back?
Witness: Yes.
Attorney: They took you outside?
Witness: Yes.
Attorney: They put you in a car?
Witness: Yes.
Attorney: A police car?
Witness: Yes.
Attorney: Pushed your head down to get you in the police car?
Witness: Yes.
Attorney: They drove away with you?
Witness: Yes.

Notice that I am telling the jury the story, much of which is based on verisimilitude. I do not know exactly how this arrest occurred, but this is the way they happen all the time. It may be routine, but it gives the jury a sense of the snitch's experience. Verisimilitude turns dry summaries of events into something that jurors see and feel.

Attorney: They drove you to the jail?
Witness: Yes.

Attorney: That's on First Avenue?
Witness: Yes.
Attorney: They brought you to the first floor?
Witness: Yes.
Attorney: Cell 111?
Witness: Yes.
Attorney: Walked you to the cell?
Witness: Yes.
Attorney: Opened the door?
Witness: Yes.
Attorney: Told you to get in?
Witness: Yes.
Attorney: You got in?
Witness: Yes.
Attorney: They closed the door?
Witness: Yes.
Attorney: The door was locked?
Witness: Yes.
Attorney: They left you there?
Witness: Yes.
Attorney: You didn't like being there? [great plausibility]

What can he say? He loved it? It was the happiest moment of his life when he got in there? We have given him a choice: agree with me or look bad. At this point, he will probably agree with you. He has now taken the first step down a slippery slope. We will continue to lead him down that slope.

Attorney: You wanted to get out?
Witness: Yes.
Attorney: You wanted to get out very much?
Witness: Yes.
Attorney: You'd do most anything to get out?
Witness: Yes.
Attorney: You would escape if you could?
Witness: Yes.
Attorney: You would cheat to get out if you could?
Witness: Yes.

Attorney: And you would steal a car to get out if you could?
Witness: Yes.

You could get either a "yes" or a "no" answer to any of these questions. At this point, I would prefer him to say "no." Normally these statements will give you control, and the witness will admit that he would escape, cheat, or steal to get out. If this witness says that he would not choose to escape after admitting that he hates being locked up, the jury will not believe him. Most of the jurors would do anything to get out of jail, too. So the snitch will probably stick with you up to this point. This brings us to our next statement.

Attorney: You would lie to get out?

The witness will pause and look at the prosecutor. He will not get any help there. The silence will continue for a short but noticeable time.

When you pose a statement like this and the witness momentarily says nothing, follow Napoleon's Third Rule of Infantry Tactics, which is also my Rule 22 of Trial Advocacy: When the enemy is in the process of destroying itself, do not interfere. Do not say anything. Let the judge be the one to go after the witness. This is a good moment for you. Relish the silence. To the jury, this kind of silence speaks stronger than any words you could say. The witness is losing credibility. Every witness who delays an answer or does not respond loses credibility.

Eventually you will get an answer. If he says he would lie to get out, then you can continue to make the point that this is exactly what he is doing. If he says that he would not lie to get out, then we have a plausibility situation. Either way, the point has been brought home to the jury in properly dramatic fashion. Again, his denial to this plausibility statement will benefit you more than control.

The System, Part III: Control

9

In the introduction, we noted that one of the things that make cross-examination difficult is the witness. If your opponent has called a witness to the stand, it is because she believes that the witness will help her case and hurt yours. The witness will often have a personal interest in frustrating the interests of your client. Therefore, for cross-examination to be helpful to your cause, you must make sure that the witness does not continue to hurt you while you are cross-examining him. This demands that you be able to control the witness.

Remember, control is not our primary goal. Our primary goal is still to look good. There will come a time in this system when we give the witness a choice between being controlled or looking like an idiot. (Plausibility cross-examination is a good example.) At that point, we prefer that the witness look bad; control is not our ultimate goal, but still it is important.

We all intuitively know what it means to control a witness. A witness is under control when he is saying what we want him to say. This is best accomplished by limiting the witness to monosyllabic answers. A witness is not under control when he is saying what he wants to say. For that matter, a witness is not under control if he is saying anything but "yes" or "no." Through our system, we can obtain total and complete control of the witness. You, the cross-examiner, will be telling your story, and the witness, totally unnecessary save for the legal requirement that he be in the witness box as you tell your story, will be simply saying "yes" or "no."

Recall the Duke Study, which distinguishes between witnesses who speak in the "narrative" mode and witnesses who are in the "fragmented" mode. Those in the narrative mode are telling us something. Importantly, they are accorded the great gift of credibility. Conversely, witnesses who present in the fragmented mode lose credibility. This distinction tells us much. It tells us that on direct examination, we want our witnesses in the narrative mode. On cross-examination, we want the witnesses in the fragmented mode. In other words, on cross-examination we want to control the witness and limit him or her to monosyllabic responses.

The result: Your cross-examination will be a preliminary closing argument. The witness will be not unlike Pavlov's dog. When you ring the bell (make your statement), the dog or witness will be programmed to give the appropriate and desired response—a simple yes or no.

A word of caution: Do not attempt to control through abrasiveness. Herein lies the closest that cross-examination gets to being an art. Simply stated, you must dominate the witness without appearing domineering. You can do this by using the system. Short statements will produce the desired control.

A. PACE

When you are cross-examining, it is important to keep up a decent pace. This will get easier as you gain more experience. Your statements should promptly follow the witness's answers, hopefully the simple "yes" or "no." If they do not, one of two things will happen. First, the witness may interpret your pauses as an invitation to talk more. That is not good. The other possibility is that the witness may take time to think. That is also not good. You know what you are going to cross the witness about before you start; the witness does not. Therefore, it is to your advantage to keep the pace fairly crisp; this way, the witness has less time to think. We do not want thinking witnesses. You, on the other hand, have already thought about your cross-examination. You should not need extra time to tell your story.

Several trial lawyers have told me that when I do cross-examinations, I have a natural rhythm. I am not sure exactly what they mean, but I suspect it means "pace."

B. LISTEN

Is it important that you listen to what the witness says? Usually not. If, as desired and expected, all the witness says is yes or no, there is no need to listen. Unlike with direct examination, there is no need to even pretend you are listening to the witness. As with most rules, however, there is an exception. The exception comes into play when the witness says something more than the desired one-word response. Then you must carefully listen to what the witness has said. You are listening for what I call a "Howard."

Howard Weitzman practices law in Los Angeles. Besides being a wonderful human being, he is a great lawyer. Among his many successes were the acquittals of John DeLorean, first in the well-publicized narcotics case tried in Los Angeles and then in the little-publicized but far more difficult and demanding bankruptcy fraud case tried in Detroit. Howard is the real thing.

Tempering this deserved praise, I must, with both embarrassment and hesitation, explain that Howard does not follow my system of cross-examination. Indeed, he violates it as much as anyone I know.[1] Howard uses open-ended questions. How else could you justify and explain his taking 17 days to cross-examine an FBI case agent?

To accomplish what he does the way he does it, you must conclude he is a genius. Possibly, like Babe Ruth, he prepares with hot dogs and beer!

Not surprisingly, his open-ended questions invite and indeed provoke long narrative responses. Howard will dissect that response and distill from it a word or phrase that he likes. He will then, with great delight, use that word or phrase like a stick. He does not use the stick to hit the witness; rather, he sticks it in the witness's right ear, pounds it in,

---

1. For this reason, many talented and experienced criminal defense lawyers with whom I teach strongly urged me not to mention Howard, and in particular the way he cross-examines.

and then pulls it out the left ear. Then he grabs both ends of the stick and, for the next few minutes, few hours, or few days, he moves the witness's head in the direction he would like it to go. When he is finished he breaks off the ends of the stick and throws them away, leaving the middle of the stick in the witness's head. He then asks another open-ended question to look for another opportunity to use a stick.

This is not something you should try unless, of course, you are also a genius and possess Howard's unique ability to make a silk purse out of a sow's ear. Needless to say, this is not a method or a system of cross-examination that can be taught. Nor, obviously, is it one that should be used.

Why, then, mention that which is contrary to everything this book teaches? Because occasionally, regardless of our abilities, the witness will decide to do a narrative. When this happens, you must listen for possible "Howards," helpful words or phrases the witness might say. Again, this is not necessarily easy to do.

To illustrate: When the Howard comes, do not use it immediately. First, you must "punish the puppy" for tinkling—for using the narrative. Having "tweaked" the puppy so as to regain control, you are ready to claim your Howard. When you start to make claim to your Howard, you might want to write the favorable word or phrase on the blackboard. You will also want to loop your Howard.

Imagine a suppression hearing where you would like to show that the police had no probable cause to search the trunk of your Johnny's car after he was pulled over for having a broken taillight, one that had been broken before or one that was more recently broken, with the glass on the ground at the scene. Assume that the police officer is Caucasian and your client is not.

Attorney: I want to ask you some questions about what happened when you pulled over the car on October 14. You understand?
Witness: Yes.
Attorney: You were on duty?
Witness: Yes.
Attorney: In the eleventh district?
Witness: Yes.
Attorney: You were in your squad car?
Witness: Yes.

Attorney: You were driving on Sacramento Avenue?
Witness: Yes.
Attorney: Going south?
Witness: Yes.
Attorney: Near Diversey Avenue?
Witness: Yes.
Attorney: You were watching the traffic?
Witness: Yes.
Attorney: You saw a car?
Witness: Yes.
Attorney: A Chevy Nova?
Witness: Yes.
Attorney: Green?
Witness: Yes.
Attorney: The Nova was stopped at the stoplight?
Witness: Yes.
Attorney: And it is your story that the taillight was broken?
Witness: Yes.
Attorney: You pulled up behind the car?
Witness: Yes.
Attorney: And you told the driver to pull over?
Witness: Yes.
Attorney: And he did?
Witness: Yes.
Attorney: You got out of your squad car?
Witness: Yes.
Attorney: And you walked to the green Nova?
Witness: Yes.
Attorney: You told the driver to get out of the car?
Witness: Yes.
Attorney: You had never seen the driver before?
Witness: No.
Attorney: You had never arrested him before?
Witness: No.
Attorney: You had no knowledge of him being in any gang?
Witness: No.
Attorney: And you had no knowledge that he had a criminal record?

Witness: No counselor, I didn't. Look, you're tellin' a pretty nice story here. But let me explain how I knew to search this guy. I've been working this district for a lot of years. I know these streets. I have a sense for how these people operate.

This police officer has just given you a Howard: "these people." A phrase like that can be used to make him appear prejudiced. Given the fact that this officer had no objective reason to search your client's car, "these people" can be rubbed in his face.

Let us see how a Howard is employed. The police officer has used the phrase "these people." First off, you want to "tweak" the puppy.

Attorney: You had no knowledge of him *being in any gang?*
Witness: Actually, no.

Now you are ready to claim your Howard. You will use the looping tool to do so.

Attorney: But you did know he was one of "*these people*"?
Witness: Yes.
Attorney: And you know how "*these people*" operate?
Witness: Yes.
Attorney: You can sense what "*these people*" are up to?
Witness: Yes.
Attorney: You can sense how one of "*these people*" operate even if you've never met this particular person?
Witness: Yes.
Attorney: And that's because "*these people*" are members of gangs?
Witness: Yes.
Attorney: But you did not know if Johnny was a member of a gang?
Witness: That's right.
Attorney: But you knew he was one of "*these people.*"
Witness: Yes.
Attorney: And "*these people*" are members of gangs?
Witness: Yes.

Attorney: You know "*these people*" commit crimes?
Witness: Yes.
Attorney: Your sense told you Johnny was committing a crime?
Witness: Yes.
Attorney: And it was your sense that caused you to stop the Nova?
Witness: Yes.
Attorney: Because he, whom you never met and knew nothing about, was one of "*these people*"?
Witness: Yes.
Attorney: "*These people*" are different than you?
Witness: Of course.

You have shown the judge that "these people" is a general reflection of this police officer's attitude toward people different from himself. It will be difficult for the judge to uphold this search.

One of my favorites is where the witness tells you he would do anything to stay out of jail. Actually, this does not usually arise as a Howard, but it might. Write "things you would do to stay out of jail." Then you cross him about those things.

Let's talk about some of the things you would do to stay out of jail.
You would cheat to stay out of jail?
You would steal a car to stay out of jail?
You would escape to stay out of jail?
You would lie to stay out of jail?

These are invaluable plausibility cross-examination questions.

Impeach

When you are invited to cross-examine a witness, you can do one of three things. You will usually do a combination of the last two.

First, you may waive your right to cross-examine. Occasionally, though rarely, this is a possibility. When done, it is usually accompanied by a totally improper and gratuitous comment, such as "This witness has not hurt us, so we have no need to cross-examine him."

Second, you may cross on what the witness said on direct. More specifically, you may cross on the "subject matter of the direct." Judges, for good reason, are liberal in interpreting the scope of this type of cross.

Third, you may, in the words of the rule, cross on "matters affecting credibility." This is legal-speak for your right to impeach. Actually, impeachment goes beyond credibility. It extends to your showing that the witness is mistaken, a liar, has reason to shade the truth, or is simply a bad person.

Impeachment, when done properly, is your opportunity to use "weapons of mass destruction." You will be able to punish the puppy far more severely than by merely tweaking it.

Obviously, you will impeach by using this system. What you can do, ways you can impeach, and how to impeach are a major topic unto themselves. When I finish this book, I intend to start a second book covering the 13 ways to impeach and how to use them.

D. THE INTRACTABLE WITNESS

Using our system, it will be difficult, but not impossible, for the witness to improperly respond or go into the narrative mode.

What should you do when you have an intractable witness?

Attorney: You saw a car?

Witness: Well, it was raining out, and I had a bag of groceries. I was trying to get my umbrella open and I was concerned the eggs might spill.

Obviously, you cannot allow this to happen. Your puppy has just tinkled. You must do something to stop it. How do we go about this?

Over the years there have been several suggestions. Most make little or no sense. For instance:

What not to do

1. When starting your cross, instruct the witness ". . . that all of my questions can be answered yes or no. Please answer with a simple yes or no."

You would give up primacy for this? Not only does this not create a good impression, it creates a bad impression. You come off as the overbearing lawyer. In other words, you are seeking to dominate the witness by being domineering.

2. As soon as the witness answers in the narrative, you reprimand him or her with a terse "just answer yes or no."

Though better than the last suggestion, this lacks elegance. Again, this is domineering and you certainly do not look good.

3. Interrupt the witness during his or her narrative. This is usually done by telling the witness to simply answer your question.

The Duke Study concluded that lawyers who interrupt witnesses, even their own, lose points with jurors. Interrupting a witness is a no-no. (Later we will talk about how we might, short of interruption, get them to stop talking.)

4. "Your Honor, would you instruct the witness to simply answer yes or no?"

With all of the tools available to you as a cross-examiner, you do not need help from the judge. As criminal defense lawyers, we have still another problem: judges are not necessarily "user-friendly" to us. Besides, if successful, all you will have done is to get the judge to "beat up" on the witness for you. This would not look good.

5. "Your Honor, I move to strike the witness's answer as being non-responsive."

Interestingly, although it is done all the time, "the opponent may not object to a non-responsive answer on that ground alone; he may move to strike such an answer if it is objectionable for any other reasons." *Elyria-Lorain Broad. Co. v. Lorain Journal Co.*, 298 F.2d 356, 359 (6th Cir. 1961). Once again, if successful, you will have succeeded only in getting the judge to beat up on the witness. Also, you have drawn attention to precisely what you did not want the jurors to hear—the non-responsive answer.

(As an aside, I have always wondered whether requesting a "motion to strike" would not constitute a violation of the federal Court Reporters Act, which prohibits striking anything from the transcript. *See* 28 U.S.C. 753.)

6. "Your Honor, I request a cautionary instruction instructing the jurors to disregard the last answer."

Most experienced trial lawyers, and for that matter most trial judges, realize the folly of this objection and the uselessness of a cautionary instruction, often referred to as "they did not see the purple elephant" instruction. Most appellate judges do not.

Besides beating up on the witness, the judge, in giving a cautionary instruction, will necessarily highlight the very testimony you did not want the jury to hear. The jury gets the idea that what the witness just said was important. Moreover, the judge's cautionary instruction may even "loop" the testimony into the jury box.

"Ladies and gentlemen, I now instruct you to disregard and not consider the witness's last statement that the president of the plaintiff corporation is a convicted felon." In effect, "Ladies and gentlemen, you did not see a large purple elephant."

Appropriately, this is one of my favorite quotes: "The naive assumption that prejudicial effects can be overcome by instructions to the jury, all practicing lawyers know to be unmitigated fiction." *Krulewitch v. United States*, 336 U.S. 440, 453 (1949) (Jackson, J., concurring) (internal citations omitted).

What You May Want to Do

I have seen reasonably effective methods used to train the puppy, though I confess that their effectiveness is, in major part, the result of the consummate skill of the lawyers who use them. A few examples follow.

"I am sorry I confused you, let me try again?" The original statement or question, which was anything but confusing, is then repeated. This is most effectively done by Juanita Brooks, an incredibly able California trial lawyer. As effective as it is, I do not believe it fits my size or personality. Juanita is petite, vivacious, and always pleasant. I know of many other lawyers, including my son Terry, who use it well. (No, Terry is not petite or vivacious, but he, like Juanita, is usually pleasant.) The only problem is that it does not lend itself to constant repetition. You can only be so nice for so long.

Gerry Spence, while writing his original question on the blackboard and pointing to it, asks, "Can you try to answer my question?"

Garvin Isaacs, a highly successful and wonderful trial lawyer from Oklahoma, most effectively says, "You came to tell us the truth. If the simple truth is yes, can't you just tell us yes?"

One of Chicago's great contributions to trial advocacy, R. Eugene Pincham, likes to get the puppy's attention by following up the tinkle with "What did I ask you?"

Appreciating the ability of these wonderful trial lawyers, these devices work well for them. In truth, all of these devices, in one way or another, reflect the particular personalities and skills of the lawyer using them. If you have a particular personality or skill, you may be able to create your own control device. Many of you can use one or more of the above-mentioned devices. However, most of us need something simple—something we, regardless of personality, can successfully use.

What about simply interrupting the witness? Never. The Duke Study, as well as manners and common sense, tells us that interrupting a witness, even your own witness on direct, creates a bad impression in the jury box. It comes off as rude and unacceptable.

That sounds reasonable, but what if the witness decides to give a long dissertation? What should you do? You still should not interrupt. You should realize that, in all probability, the witness is, like most long-winded people, boring the jury. This is another example where, by denying you control, the witness looks bad—an even better result.

Violating my own admonition not to tell war stories, I share an experience. A few years back, I was cross-examining an expert witness who apparently had been vaccinated by a phonograph needle. He loved to talk, on and on. For that matter, as was his nature, he did so on direct. It was all too obvious that the very able prosecutor was less than pleased with his rambling. Try as she might, she could not curtail his run-on answers.

The young lawyer trying the case with me told me he believed in my cross-examination system, but feared it would not work on this particular witness.

I purposely started the cross-examination with the shortest and simplest statements I could think of. This initially had little result "controlling" the witness. His answers were at least 10 times longer than my statements. Looking at others in the courtroom, particularly the jury, I could not help but notice their displeasure with the witness. For that matter, the most displeased person in the courtroom was the suffering prosecutor. She knew the long-winded witness was turning the jury off.

Some 10 to 15 minutes into my cross, the witness, a decent and obviously an intelligent man, suddenly realized the effect he was having. He then changed and became a wonderful "yes" and "no" witness. (He gave me total control but stopped "looking bad.") Maybe I would have been better off without the control, except that his answers were making my case.

The best way to stop the run-on witness is to no longer look at him. Turn your back on him while he continues to talk. Pick up a piece of paper and give the appearance of reading it. Of course you are *not* reading it, you are listening for "Howards."

Most people stop talking when the person they are talking to is obviously not listening. Once the talking stops, usually when you turn away, slowly re-engage the witness by simply restating the original statement—tweaking the tinkling puppy.

Let us now talk specifically about how you control the verbose witness—or train a tinkling puppy.

Attorney: You saw a car?

Witness: Well, it was raining out and I had a bag of groceries. I was trying to get my umbrella open and I was concerned the eggs might spill.

This is an example of the big tinkle. There are small tinkles that also demand punishment. Small tinkles would include "Yes, I think so"; "If you say so"; and "I'd have to agree with that."

There are also acceptable though not desired answers, such as "yeah," "uh-huh," and "that's right." The problem with these answers is that they tend to distract the jury from listening to your story. Still, they probably do not justify punishing the puppy. When the puppy has tinkled on the floor, however, you must punish him. What about going over and punching him in the face, or possibly kicking him in the butt? Hardly. These methods would offend and be inconsistent with our "look good" purpose.

Instead, we will merely "tweak" the offending puppy. We will roll up a newspaper and tweak or hit the puppy across the nose. (Obviously, this is an analogy. We must not have physical contact with the witness.) How do you "tweak" the puppy? Simply repeat—word for word—your original statement.

Attorney: You saw a car?

When repeating the statement, you must do two things, and maybe a third.

1. Your repetition will be said *slower* than the pace you were using (this is done for emphasis).
2. You will use a *rising inflection* on the last word in your repeat statement. In our illustration, you will overemphasize by stating the last word louder: *CAR*. This important rising inflection tells the witness that a specific answer is required.

   Usually, when done properly, this will do the trick. If the repeat or tweak does not get the desired result—the simple "yes"—but rather results in additional tinkle (it will be less than the first tinkle):
3. Simply repeat the tweak. Again, do so slowly with the rising inflection, but this time, start with the witness's name (this is the one exception to the rule that we do not refer to witness by their names or honorifics).[3]

Attorney: Mrs. Smith, you saw a CAR?

Not only will this usually do the trick, but you will have gained more than you would have had the witness simply said "yes" the first time around. The yes answer would have earned you your gold star, but the evasiveness of the witness will have made her "look bad."

This point is best made by explaining how FBI special agents at Quantico are trained to be witnesses. (Their training is excellent, and by and large they make exceptionally good and credible witnesses.) They are taught not to fight the cross-examiner when the cross-examiner is correct. Specifically, they are instructed to answer with the simple "yes." Of course, this instruction does not apply if the cross-examiner is foolish enough to ask an open-ended question. If you ask an open-ended question of a special agent, you might as well leave the courtroom and go out and get a beer. The special agent will probably take some time to tell his story—one that will ensure the defendant's conviction.

---

3. Bob Hirsch, an exceptionally talented Arizona trial lawyer, has taken this one step further. He effectively uses not merely the first and last name, but the middle name as well.

For that matter, it is my understanding that experienced and competent civil trial lawyers, similar to the FBI training, "woodshed" their witnesses to simply answer "yes" or "no" and not to fight with the cross-examiner. Again, this is good advice. Appreciating this also helps you when you use the system.

Is it possible that even after the third "tweak" the puppy will still tinkle? Possible, yes; probable, no. What do we do when the possible does happen? Should you continue to "tweak" the puppy? Probably not, as you will begin to bore both judge and jury. You must continue on. Actually, you will have won this skirmish; the witness will have looked bad—more specifically, evasive. Still, we are not totally satisfied. We do not like our puppies tinkling. A little post punishment is in order.

Attorney: You saw a car?
Witness: Well, it was raining out and I had a bag of groceries. I was trying to get my umbrella open and I was concerned the eggs might spill.
Attorney: You saw a CAR?
Witness: Well, it was raining out and I had a bag of groceries. I was trying to get my umbrella open and I was concerned the eggs might spill.
Attorney: Mrs. Smith: . . . you . . . saw . . . a . . . CAR?
Witness: Well, that rain made it a bit difficult to see.
Attorney: But you did see something?
Witness: Yes.
Attorney: You saw Tom Clancy?
Witness: Yes.
Attorney: He was driving a car?
Witness: Yes.
Attorney: You saw that car? (This is what you wanted.)
Witness: Yes.
Attorney: So you did see a car?
Witness: Yes.
Attorney: The *car you saw* was green? (Loop underscored)
Witness: Yes.
Attorney: The *car you saw* was a convertible?
Witness: Yes.
Attorney: The *car you saw* was a Pontiac?
Witness: Yes.

The jurors certainly know now that the puppy saw a car. Of equal if not greater importance, the jurors know that the puppy resisted giving this answer.

It is critically important that you always tweak the puppy when it tinkles (for exceptions to this rule, see Chapter 10). Lawyers will want to explain to me that the "tinkle" did not hurt; it did not include negative material. This may be an accurate assessment of the facts but an inaccurate understanding of the system. *All tinkle is bad. It must be stopped and the tinkling puppy punished.* If you do not punish the tinkling puppy, the puppy will continue to tinkle even more and probably drop a turd or two.

E. EXCEPTIONS

Always "tweak" the tinkling puppy except for three exceptions:

1) When you were wrong or used inaccurate details.

Attorney: You saw a car?
Witness: Yes.
Attorney: The car was blue?
Witness: No, counsel, the car was light blue.

After glancing at your notes and realizing the car was in fact light blue, you have enough common sense not to "tweak" or confront the witness. This would be stupid. You must be quick of mind and must seek to retrain the puppy, rebuild your credibility, and regain your storytelling status.

Attorney: There was blue in the car?
Witness: Yes.
Attorney: But it was a light blue?
Witness: Yes.

2) When you have used a perfect one-word statement.

Attorney: You saw a car?
Witness: Yes.
Attorney: Green?
Witness: I was concerned about my groceries, I thought my eggs were going to fall.

We have an obvious problem. Repeating the term "green" slowly with a rising inflection would sound totally inelegant. The cure is to add a few additional terms not used the first time.

Attorney: You saw a car?
Witness: Yes.
Attorney: Green?
Witness: I was concerned about my groceries, I thought my eggs were going to fall.
Attorney: The car you saw was green?

3) When you are required to "tweak" the puppy a second time, you will again add terms. Specifically, you will start your statement by using the name of the witness.

Attorney: Mrs. Smith: you . . . saw . . . a . . . CAR?
Witness: Yes.

The Asked and Answered Objection

Some of you, for good or for evil, are evidence scholars. You have a slight problem with my "tweaking" repetition. What, you ask, about the objection "asked and answered"?

First, I have some good news. There is no such proper objection. There is, however, the proper objection under Federal Rule of Evidence 403, "boring." Your tweaking will not reach the boring stage. Now the bad news, which totally trumps the good news. Most judges do not know there is no such objection. They hear it and sustain it with regularity—evidence is what the judge had for breakfast, and she ate "asked and answered" cereal. It would be totally unavailing and, indeed, stupid for you, the cross-examiner, to argue to the judge that the "asked and answered" objection does not exist.

Where does this leave us? Actually, not in bad shape. Let us look at what really could happen in the courtroom.

Puppies can tinkle in one of three ways.

First Possibility

Attorney: You saw a car?
Witness: It was raining and I was concerned I would drop something from my grocery bag.
Attorney: You - saw - a - CAR?
Opponent: Objection, Your Honor, asked and answered.

Let me elevate or promote you. You are the judge. How would you rule on this objection? You would overrule the objection, as would almost all judges. The cross statement was asked but *not answered.*

Second Possibility

Attorney: You saw a car?
Witness: I don't know. I don't remember.
Attorney: You . . . saw . . . a . . . CAR?
Opponent: Objection, Your Honor, asked and answered.

Once again, how would you rule on this objection?

The answer is not as obvious or as clear-cut as the earlier situation. I have done some totally unscientific research and inquiries and, as best I can determine, about 70 percent of the judges would overrule this objection. Again, the statement was asked, and again, it was not answered. So, in a majority of the courtrooms we do not have a problem.

What about the courtrooms where the judge sustains this objection? We hardly have a problem. We were merely attempting to mildly punish the puppy by tweaking him. The judge has just told us we cannot do so. We accept this, as we must.

Still, the judge, by her ruling, has of necessity told us much more. The judge has told us we cannot mildly punish the puppy, but we can more severely punish the puppy.

The answer "I don't know. I don't remember" allows us to either *refresh the witness's recollection* or to *impeach* the witness. Refreshing recollection allows us to do more than tweak the puppy. We get to hit the puppy with a fist. If refreshing recollection does not do the trick and the puppy still does not know or remember, then we are allowed to impeach the witness. We get to select a Louisville Slugger bat and, from five steps away, run at the puppy and belt it. This gets the puppy's attention. When done properly, it is particularly effective in getting the puppy toilet-trained and in the "yes" mode. So again, we have no problem.

Third Possibility

Attorney: You saw a car?
Witness: It was raining and I was trying to get my umbrella up and I saw a car but I was more concerned about spilling my groceries.
Attorney: You - saw - a - CAR?
Opponent: Objection, your Honor, asked and answered.

This is your final chance to be the judge. Will you sustain or overrule this objection?

My unscientific research and inquiries suggests that 80 percent of the judges would sustain this objection. Does this create a flaw in the system? A flaw, yes, but not a major problem. The flaw is that you will not be able to tweak the puppy; the tinkle will go unpunished. However, the jurors will not like the way the witness answered a simple question (statement). Human nature suggests that long-winded, irrelevant responses are not well accepted. This being so, you have no major problem and can live with the flaw.

Still, I am not, nor will you be, totally satisfied with this result. Something more can and should be done with this tinkling puppy. Let us use the *looping tool* to punish the puppy.

Court: Objection sustained.
Attorney: The *car you saw* was going west?
Witness: Yes.
Attorney: You knew the driver of the *car you saw*?
Witness: Yes.
Attorney: Tom Clancy was driving the *car you saw*?

Another consideration is the witness who will not cooperate. This is usually a tinkling puppy, one who exceeds the required monosyllabic response. For a variation on this theme, what about the puppy who does not respond at all?

You use an understandable, simple statement. The puppy says nothing, or possibly nods its head. As a young lawyer, the head nodding prompted me to caustically comment that the court reporter could not record the nod of the head. The puppy, I snidely explained, had to answer orally. This was part of the "attack mode" cross, which I have long since abandoned.

Well, then, what do you do? You follow Napoleon's Third Rule of Infantry Tactics, which is my Rule 37: "When the enemy is in the process of destroying itself, do not interfere." Any witness, on direct or cross, who does not answer or even delays in answering, is losing credibility. On cross-examination, this is good. Ergo, we will remain silent and do or say nothing. This is the court's responsibility, and the judge will handle it.

There are many other things a witness might do short of being intractable, things you should be pleased to see. What are some of the mannerisms associated with not telling the truth? How about a change in voice pitch or rate of speech? Yes, but this will not be obvious if witnesses are properly in the monosyllabic response mode.

How about the use of "ums" and "ahs"? How about avoidance of eye contact? How about putting a hand to their face—in particular, their mouth? How about turning their body away or nervous movement of the feet or legs? Each affects the jury's perception of witness credibility.

F. SAFE HAVENS—WHAT TO DO WHEN YOU GET HURT

Even when you are doing the system correctly, there are going to be times when things will not go right. This is normal and consistent with Murphy's Law. Remember that the purpose of cross-examination is to look good. When things go badly and you do not look good, do not lose your composure. Never bleed in front of the jury.

There are two ways to look bad in front of a jury. The first is when you somehow hurt yourself. We try to minimize these self-inflicted wounds, but they happen. The rule is simple: Maintain composure. The second way to get hurt is when the witness hurts you. Using this system certainly minimizes this exposure. However, no matter how careful you are, sometimes the witness will manage to say something devastating during your cross-examination.

If and when this happens, there are two things you must do. The first is not to show any reaction to the jury. Face it, juries are not always inclined to pay overly close attention to exactly what was said.

Often, the only way they know that you have been hurt is if you show it. Do not do so. Even when you are cut deeply, do not bleed in front of the jury.

The second thing is to get to a safe haven immediately. In preparing for any potentially dangerous witness, you should have a safe area of cross-examination ready to move into if anything goes wrong. For example:

Attorney: Let's talk about what happened as you were walking home. You understand?
Witness: Yes.
Attorney: You walked down Fourth Street?
Witness: Yes.
Attorney: You knew that street well?
Witness: Yes.
Attorney: You knew where you were going?
Witness: Yes.
Attorney: You had a glass of wine?
Witness: Yes.
Attorney: You walked under the viaduct?
Witness: Yes.
Attorney: It was dark under the viaduct?
Witness: Yes.
Attorney: As you walked under that dark viaduct, someone leapt out at you?
Witness: Yes.
Attorney: You were surprised?
Witness: Yes.
Attorney: They grabbed your purse and ran off?
Witness: Yes.
Attorney: This took no more than a few seconds?
Witness: Yes.
Attorney: You did not know the person who grabbed your purse?
Witness: Actually, I did. It was Johnny, your client. He and I were high school classmates. We took freshman algebra together. It took me a while to remember where I knew him from, but I knew that he was familiar, and that's why I was able to remember his face.

Attorney: I am going to ask you some questions about what happened when the police showed you the lineup. You understand?

Witness: Yes.

It is hoped that will not ever happen to you. If it does, you might consider a plea. In any event, do not make it worse by wilting when it happens.

To make my point, I will tell you a story. On the night before an anticipated battle, a brave and exceptionally competent general spent hours going over every possible contingency with his senior officers. At the end of the meeting, when he had gone over and anticipated every conceivable detail of the next day's battle, the general walked over to his foot locker and pulled out a red shirt. "Gentlemen," he announced, "we have planned for everything that could happen tomorrow. Nonetheless, there are never any guarantees of victory. I will take one final precaution. If I should be wounded, I do not want the men to know I have been wounded. Therefore, I will wear this red shirt. They will not see the blood nor know I was wounded."

His senior officers marveled at the thoroughness and wisdom of this preparation. Truly they were in the presence of a military genius.

One of the senior officers, who was not quite as brave as his commanding general, stepped forward and said, "General, that is a brilliant suggestion and incredible preparation. I, too, shall dress in preparation for the worst. Before tomorrow's battle, I shall also be ready. I will wear my brown trousers."

You may forget the brown trousers part, but remember the red shirt. Always wear the red shirt when you cross-examine. Make sure the jury does not see you bleed.

Additional Considerations 10

A. POSSIBLE EXCEPTIONS TO THE SYSTEM

Earlier you were told to never ask questions on cross-examination. We have seen some applications of that system. As with all rules, however, there are a few exceptions—times when you may ask questions on cross-examination.

Some years ago, I made a list of about a half-dozen exceptions to my own rule of never asking questions. I have since rejected most of that list. I am down to two exceptions during trial. The other exceptions apply only to non-trial situations.

The first trial exception is an extremely limited one; it applies only when attempting to get something or someone characterized as either near or far, or tall or short. Suppose my client, who is 5'8", is accused of robbing a liquor store. In his statement to the police, the clerk estimated the height of the person who robbed him as 5'10". I want to make the most of this difference, which in truth is not much of a difference. I would like the clerk to characterize the robber as a "tall man." A question is required to do this. "How tall was the man who robbed you?" The witness's expressed answer should be 5'10". However, the witness adopted our characterization of "tall." We will loop the "tall."

Attorney: The TALL robber was wearing a mask?
Witness: Yes.

Attorney: The TALL robber had a beard? (Obviously, your client does not have a beard.)
Witness: Yes.
Attorney: And the TALL robber took the money?
Witness: Yes.

The difference between 5'8" and 5'10" is not of much importance. The characterization "tall" is significant. You can later argue in closing that your client, who is 5'8", is certainly not tall.

This also works with distance. Do you want the car "close" or "far"? The witness statement has the car 8 feet away. "How close was the car?" "How far away was the car?" The distance is the same, but the message is totally different. Though not as effective, you may want to ask how fast the car was going.

For criminal defense lawyers, there is a second exception that would allow the asking of a question. The absence of discovery in criminal cases and a Supreme Court decision create the circumstances for the exception.

In *Smith v. Illinois*, 390 U.S. 129 (1968), the Court held it was reversible error to deny a criminal defendant's attorney the right to cross-examine a prosecution witness on where he or she lives and his or her correct name. Obviously, there is little discovery. From this ruling it follows that, if and when necessary or helpful, a prosecution witness may be asked his or her name and address. Of course, in a more perfect situation I would prefer, assuming I knew the information, to *tell* the witness rather than *ask* him.

If we are not actually on trial but are involved in a preliminary stage of the case, a deposition in a civil case, or possibly a preliminary hearing in a criminal case, we may well want to ask questions—indeed, even open-ended questions.

This is not an absolute. Many civil lawyers have told me that on rare occasions, when they want to demonstrate to their opponent how strong their case is, they will use the system to destroy the witness. When you have a powerful case that can be best demonstrated by cross-examination, you may want to use the system. Most depositions do not allow for these opportunities. In most depositions, you will ask questions, including open-ended questions. From these usually long answers, you will obtain the raw material you can use when cross-examining at trial.

Truthfully, some criminal lawyers use evidentiary hearings like preliminary hearings and motions to suppress, not in the realistic hope they will prevail, but rather to obtain some discovery. Discovery in criminal cases is, unfortunately, limited. Where the preliminary hearing is being used with no anticipation of success but rather in aid of discovery, then questions, including open-ended questions, are in order.

B. MISDIRECTION

An interesting variation of misdirection, though not one adaptable to cross-examination, was sent to me by an outstanding trial lawyer, trial advocacy teacher, and one of my favorite persons: Charleston, South Carolina, trial lawyer Dale Cobb.

Question: You are participating in a race. You overtake the second person. What position are you in?

Answer: Many answer first place. This is wrong. You have taken the second person's place and are in second place.

Question: If you overtake the last person, what position are you in?

Answer: If you answer you are second to last, you are wrong. You cannot overtake the last person.

Question: Back to arithmetic. This is to be done in your head, unaided by a calculator, paper, or writing instrument. Take 1,000 and add 40 to it. Now add another 1,000. Now add 30. Add another 1,000. Now add 20. Now add another 1,000. Now add 10. What is the total?

Answer: Did you get 5,000? Most people do. Actually, and surprisingly, the correct answer is 4,100. Check it with a calculator!

Question: A mute person goes into a store and wants to buy a toothbrush. By imitating the action of brushing his teeth, he successfully expresses himself to the store clerk and the purchase is done. Next, a blind man comes into the store and he wants to buy a pair of sunglasses. How does he indicate what he wants?

Answer: All he has to do is open his mouth and tell the store clerk what he wants.

As a cross-examiner, you would like the witness to say what you want him or her to say, something that will help your case. The problem, of course, is that what you want said is usually not what the witness wants to say. Is there anything you can do to get your desired result?

You can, as we discussed earlier, get the witness into the "yes mode." Once a witness becomes comfortable in the "yes" mode, he or she will abandon thinking and simply answer everything "yes."

Can a cross-examiner "misdirect" a witness? If so, how? Finally, might there be practical, no less ethical, problems?

Anybody, including witnesses, can be misdirected. A wonderful example of this, one I have used with success many times, is the so-called grammar quiz. This was taught to me by a very well-regarded and successful trial lawyer from Virginia and Washington, D.C., John Lowe.

The Grammar Quiz

Start by asking for an exceptionally bright person to volunteer to take your grammar quiz. I usually ask for an Ivy League graduate or someone with a Jesuit education. This will also work with a single person, though it is more fun with a group.

Explain to your volunteer that you will ask three *grammar* questions. He or she is to answer aloud. The rest of the group should answer silently. The objective, you explain, is to see if anyone answers all three grammar questions correctly.

First *grammar* question: Which is correct: *You and I* went to the store or *You and me* went to the store? Volunteer answers out loud.

Second *grammar* question: Which is correct: Two and two *is* eight or two and two *are* eight? Over 90 percent of the time, your volunteer will answer "Two and two are eight." There will be no laughter, as everybody will have been misled. There will be no third grammar question;[1] instead, you will dismissively tell the volunteer that he or she is a dummy, that when you went to school you learned that two and two are four. Believe me, when done orally, this works. Why?

When you explained the quiz, you emphasized it as a *grammar* quiz. This becomes the focus and concern of the volunteer; the math accuracy is obfuscated.

1. John Lowe does ask additional "misleading" questions. They are not grammar questions, but they are great examples of how to mislead.

We can, with a punctilio of care and even then with obvious risk, similarly "misdirect" a witness by emphasizing the unimportant and underemphasizing what you are after.

Example: Defense of a Rape Case

For many years now, the National Criminal Defense College, an outstanding place to learn trial advocacy, and indeed much more, has used an alleged rape case as one of its four cases. Details of the case are unnecessary. Suffice it to say that the defendant does not or, at least, certainly should not deny having had sex with his co-worker. The defense has to be consent or, as the facts allow, "confusion."

In brainstorming the case, the participants agree they do not want the co-worker witness using the term "rape." (This should be addressed with a motion *in limine*.) The terms the defense attorneys would like to use and see used are "had sex" and "made love." The defense attorney can and will use these euphemistic terms, but what about getting the co-worker witness to use them? Here misdirection could work.

The co-worker witness emphasized on direct examination that the defendant held both of her wrists. Realistically, the witness will not back off or change the "held the wrist" direct unless, of course, you have Perry Mason representing the defendant. That said, repeating this on cross, though usually not advisable, would not be totally destructive where a greater good might be achieved.

During cross, the defense attorney can use misdirection as follows:

Q: HE HELD BOTH OF YOUR WRISTS while you had sex?
A: Yes.
Q: HE HELD BOTH OF YOUR WRISTS while you made love?
A: Yes.

Obviously, there is some risk; indeed, misdirection always involves some risk. The witness could reply with "we did not make love, he raped me." Yet I can and do report to you that, over many years of working with this problem at the College, it has always worked much like the "two and two are eight" misdirection. Not only has it worked, one time it worked against all odds, where the witness *knew* exactly what to expect and was resolved not to be misdirected.

Some years ago, a talented and totally dedicated young actress, Denise de LaRue, after several years of working as an actress at the College Summer Sessions, became the coordinator of the wonderful actors and actresses who contribute much to the success of the College. According to the schedule, she came into my section in midmorning the day we were doing cross-examinations. She was and remains a good friend.

She came in the room prepared to play one of the women witnesses in the four problems we were using. She pleasantly told the group that they were indeed fortunate because they would be the best cross-examiners in the building by the end of the day—that my system and how I taught it would guarantee this. To say the least, this pleased me and helped me get the attention and confidence of the group.

She then turned to me and, with a total change in disposition, emphatically announced that none of the female actresses playing the co-worker would agree they "had sex" or "made love." She had specifically instructed and warned them of the probability that our group would try misdirection. She further explained she had put a sign, which was not to be removed, on the door of our room as a reminder to her actresses.

Based on past success, I bet her two martinis we would get one of her actresses to agree to the terms "had sex" or "made love" before the day was finished. Having made me promise not to remove her sign, she agreed to the bet. As fate would have it, the next lawyer up to do a cross had the alleged rape case. He did an outstanding job and yes, he got Denise, using misdirection, to agree they "had sex" and "made love." After he appropriately looped (repeated the important terms) a second time, Denise realized what had just happened. She became enraged and, expressing unkind words, stormed out of the room. A minute or two later, she regained her cool and returned to the room to finish the cross. She proclaimed that indeed we had tricked her—which was accurate. Then again, we tricked her with something she was both aware of and determined to not allow—misdirection.

As a pleasant follow-up, the participant who did the outstanding cross-examination was then an assistant public defender in LaCrosse, Wisconsin. Now a judge, Dale Pasell is, I am sure, as excellent a judge as he was a defender.

Denise de LaRue is now a lawyer who, with great skill, specializes in jury selection. And yes, I did get my two martinis, and we remain good friends.

C. ETHICAL CONSIDERATIONS

We talk about getting witnesses into the "yes" mode so they will simply and automatically answer "yes" to our statements. We also talk about misdirection and suggest that where it is used, we can, in effect, trick the witness into a wrong answer.

Are we ethically allowed to do this on cross-examination? Truthfully, I am not sure of the correct answer to this question. The law is unclear. We start with Rule 3.3 of the American Bar Association *Model Rules of Professional Conduct*. The rule prohibits a lawyer from knowingly offering evidence the lawyer knows is false. An argument could be made that a cross-examining lawyer is not "offering evidence" in the sense meant by the rule. The witness is not your witness.

The American Bar Association *Criminal Justice Standards*, which concern the trial of criminal cases, addresses this issue. Prosecution Function Standard 3-5.7(d) states: "It is unprofessional conduct for a (prosecutor) lawyer to ask a question which implies the existence of a factual predicate for which a good faith belief is lacking." A little less restrictive is Defense Function Standard 4-7.6 (b): "A lawyer's belief or knowledge that the witness is telling the truth does not preclude cross-examination but should, if possible, be taken into consideration by counsel in conducting the cross-examination."

The case law suggests a far more liberal standard. The United States Supreme Court, in both a dissenting and concurring opinion by Justice White, said that a criminal "defense counsel has no . . . obligation to ascertain and present the truth." *United States v. Wade*, 388 U.S. 218, 256 (1967) (White, J., dissenting in part and concurring in part). "Undoubtedly, there are some limits that defense counsel must observe, but more often than not, defense counsel will cross-examine a prosecution witness and impeach him if he can, even if he thinks the witness is telling the truth, just as he will attempt to destroy a witness who he thinks is lying." *Id.* at 258.

> Law enforcement officers have the obligation to convict the guilty and to make sure they do not convict the innocent. They must be dedicated to making the criminal trial a procedure for the ascertainment of the true facts surrounding the commission of the crime. To this extent, our so-called adversary system is not adversary at all; nor should it be. But defense counsel

> has no comparable obligation to ascertain and present the truth. Our system assigns him a different mission. He must be and is interested in preventing the conviction of the plea of guilty, we must also insist that he defend his client whether he is innocent or guilty. The state has the obligation to present the evidence. He need not present any witnesses to the police, or reveal any confidences of his client, or furnish any other information to help the prosecutor's case. If he can confuse a witness, even a truthful one, or make him appear at a disadvantage, unsure or indecisive, that will be his normal course. Our interest in not convicting the innocent permits counsel to put the state to its proof, to put the state's case in the worst possible light, regardless of what he thinks or knows to be the truth.

United States v. Wade, 388 U.S. 218, 256, 257, 258 (1967) (Justice White, concurring and dissenting).

The Seventh Circuit gives us mixed messages. In *United States v. Elizonso,* the court states: "A prosecutor may not ask a question which implies a factual predicate which the examiner knows he cannot support by evidence . . . ." *United States v. Elizondo*, 920 F.2d 1308, 1313 (7th Cir. 1990).

However, in *United States v. Phillips,* the court, without citation, follows Justice White's reasoning in *Wade*. The appealing defendant (a perjury conviction) argued that the prosecutor did not cross-examine to establish the truth. The court's language, strikingly similar to that in *Wade,* said: "The point of impeachment, however, is not to vouch for the validity of the impeachment material: rather, it is to suggest that the witness may be mistaken or inconsistent in his testimony and therefore is not a credible witness." *United States v. Phillips*, 914 F.2d 835, 839 (7th Cir. 1990).

In sum, this confusion suggests extreme caution. Most of the time you will not be certain that your desired facts are inaccurate. Then you have no problem. In those rare instances where you absolutely know the facts you want elicited are inaccurate, you may want to look more to the ethical pronouncements than the language of the case law.

11 Why the System Works

The system works for three reasons:

1. It allows the cross-examiner to tell a story, the most effective method of persuasion and memory retention. People remember more details in a story than if presented with an equal number of random facts.
2. It allows the cross-examiner to make a good impression. It is generally accepted that when one watches a TV message, when the speaker is finished the viewer has probably forgotten the substance of the message, but the good or bad impression of the speaker is remembered.
3. It allows the cross-examiner to reasonably control the witness without the asperity of traditional cross-examination. To do this, the system uses cultural and societal norms (head nods, short statements, and occasional minor punishment) to evoke short, monosyllabic answers. The witness, to avoid "looking bad," will go along with the program or suffer even greater embarrassment.

Obviously, just as each case is different, so also is each lawyer different. We have different personalities and different strengths and weaknesses. When trying a case and, it follows, when we cross-examine, we must take these differences into consideration.

I suggest you first learn the system. That accomplished, you can and should make changes to better fit your individual personality. For instance, I like to conclude a transition with the phrase "you understand." I know many excellent trial lawyers who use the system who are not comfortable with that phrase. They, as well they should, use something different.

In the final analysis, you want to make sure you are in major part following the system and that, when cross-examining, you are "looking good," telling your "story" by using "short statements."

Appendix: Examples of Cross-Examination

The following cross-examinations are from actual cases. The lawyer conducting the cross-examination is listed. However, these cross-examinations have been edited. More specifically, the names of persons, except for the attorney doing the cross-examination, and places have been changed.

Cross-examination of a psychiatrist in a federal bank robbery by Terence F. MacCarthy, Chicago, Illinois

Q It would be fair to say that Robert Rice has a history of serious mental illness?
A Yes.
Q And that history of serious illness goes back to 1986?
A As far as I know it does, right.
Q That history of serious mental illness goes back to 1986?
A Yes, that is what I put in my report.
Q So it goes back till 1986?
A Yes.
Q Around May of 1986?
A I don't remember the precise date of it.
Q It was May of 1986?
A Yes. Again, that's what I put in my report.
Q So it was May of 1986?
A Yes.
Q Now, I want to ask you about what happened to Robert Rice in 1986, you understand?
A Yes, I understand.
Q He had a job?
A Yes, he did.
Q Selling insurance?
A Yes.
Q For the International Insurance Company.
A Yes.
Q He was married?
A Yes.
Q He had been married a few years?
A Yes.
Q And a son was born in 1986?
A Yes.
Q In February of 1986?

A Yes.

Q February 4?

A Yes.

Q About three months after his son was born Robert Rice's world suddenly collapsed?

A I don't remember the specific date of that, but he told me that that's in essence what happened to him.

Q Sometime in 1986 his world collapsed?

A Yes.

Q He became mentally ill?

A He sure did.

Q His mental illness was a very serious one?

A Yes, indeed.

Q Schizophrenia?

A Yes, it was.

Q This is what caused his world to collapse?

A It was part, part of it.

Q This is what caused his world to collapsed?

A Yes. Indeed.

Q I want to ask you some questions about schizophrenia. You understand?

A Okay.

Q It is fair to say that medical experts are not sure as to what causes schizophrenia?

A Not precisely, no, but we've got some pretty good ideas.

Q But you are not sure?

A Not precisely, no.

Q There are different theories as to what may cause schizophrenia?

A There are.

Q One theory holds that it is genetically caused?

A There is evidence to support that and a considerable body of it.

Q So one theory holds that it is genetically caused?

A Yes. Indeed.

Q That would mean one would be born with the genes that caused schizophrenia?

A Yes.

Q The schizophrenic would not be responsible for having those genes?

A That's right.

Q Some others believe that it is caused by chemical imbalance?

A The concept is that the chemical imbalance is probably a genetic factor.

Q So some believe that it is caused by a chemical imbalance?

A Yes, that's my understanding.

Q The schizophrenic is not responsible for that chemical imbalance?

A That would be correct.

Q I want to ask you some questions about neurotransmitters, you understand?

A Yes.

Q Some believe neurotransmitters may be the cause of schizophrenia.

A Well, that's—that seems to be what the research is showing, that neurotransmitter plays an integral part in the expression of the disease known as schizophrenia.

Q So some believe neurotransmitters may be the cause?

A Okay.

Q Neurotransmitters can be analyzed chemically?

A Oh, yes.

Q Again the schizophrenic is not responsible for his having neurotransmitters.

A Of course not.

Q And there is still another theory, that schizophrenia may be caused by a trauma?

A Yes.

Q For instance, a severe hit on the head?

A Yes.

Q Some folks believe that?

A Yes.

Q Incidentally, you know that Robert Rice did have a major trauma when he was in high school?

A He fell some 70 feet off a bridge.

Q So he had a major trauma when he was in high school?

A Yes. He fell 70 feet and hurt himself seriously. I understand that he was never unconscious as a result of that, which was rather surprising. He got some fractures of , I think, a wrist and an ankle. I'm not sure that he was ever reported as having been unconscious.

Q He had a major trauma in high school?

A Yes.

Q In any event, whatever caused Robert Rice's schizophrenia, he got it?

A Yes.

Q And whatever caused his schizophrenia he was not responsible for.

A Yes.

Q Now, I want to ask you a few questions about his earlier delusions, the 1986 delusions. You understand?

A Yes.

Q Robert Rice told you he was taken over?

A He told me that he had been given something in his coffee at work that had an effect on his body, that a packet of some sort had been inserted by his drinking that coffee and that it extended tubes in his brain and his bowels, and that he was controlled by a computer and that his eye had been replaced with a 120 millimeter camera, like a television camera.

Q Robert Rice told you he had been taken over?

A Yes, that's what he told me.

Q He told you a computer controlled him?

A Yes.

Q He told you that this was caused by drinking coffee?

A Yes, sir.

Q Coffee he got at work?

A It was caused by something in the coffee that was served at work, yes, sir.
Q He got the coffee at work?
A Yes, sir.
Q He thought somebody put a packet in that coffee?
A Yes.
Q This caused him to defecate?
A It caused him to defecate his brains out his rectum.
Q So it caused him to defecate?
A Yes.
Q He defecated his brains out his rectum?
A Yes.
Q And he told you he had his eye removed?
A No, he didn't say he had his eyes removed. He said his eye had been replaced by his camera device.
Q The camera was placed where his eye should have been?
A Yes.
Q The camera replaced the eye?
A Yes, sir.
Q So the eye had to be removed to be replaced by the camera.
A That's what I said, yes.
Q The eye was replaced by a camera?
A Yes, sir.
Q So the eye was removed?
A Yes.
Q Now, you were satisfied, that these things really did not happen?
A Of course.
Q Robert Rice, believed these delusions?
A That's the nature of a delusion.
Q So he believed them?
A These were his perceptions of reality, yes, sir.
Q So he believed them?
A Yes.
Q They were his reality?

A His reality was that was in fact in place at the time, which were not any of those devices. His perceptions of reality were as he described them.

Q These to him were the way he saw reality?

A Yes.

Q This was part of his world?

A Yes.

Q His reality?

A Yes.

Q I want to ask you some questions about what happened after this first serious attack of schizophrenia in 1986. You understand?

A Yes.

Q His wife left him?

A She did.

Q She took his son with her?

A She did.

Q He lost his job?

A Yes, he did.

Q He moved in with his parents?

A Yes.

Q It would be fair to say, that his parents, Mr. and Mrs. Rice, then lived with him through most of his serious illness?

A Yes.

Q I want to ask you some questions about Robert Rice's admission to Memorial Hospital on April 1st of 1987. You understand?

A I understand you're going to ask me some questions about the admission, yes.

Q You know of that admission?

A I don't know the precise date.

Q But you know of that admission?

A Yes.

Q You learned of that admission after you examined Robert Rice?

A Yes.

Q But you did not learn of that admission until after you left Minnesota?

A That's right.
Q And after Robert Rice had left Minnesota?
A Yes.
Q When you examined Robert Rice, you did not know about any of his outpatient visits?
A No.
Q You did not know about his hospitalizations?
A Not specifically, no.
Q You did not know that in early 1989 Robert Rice was going in for medication as an outpatient at least twice, sometimes three times a month?
A No.
Q You did not know he was receiving a schizophrenic drug, Prolixin?
A No.
Q You did not know that his last medication was on July 6th, of 1989?
A No, I did not.
Q I want to ask you what happens when a schizophrenic stops taking Prolixin?
A Sure.
Q It would be fair to say that within several months that medication would have worn off?
A Well, that medication is expected to last or have its effect for anywhere between two and six weeks. After that it may linger for a considerable period of time, but the level of it is insufficient to have any clinical effect.
Q So after several months it would have worn off?
A Yes.
Q As that medication starts to wear off the ravages of schizophrenia start to take over?
A Yes.
Q The schizophrenia can go into the prodromal stage?
A Yes.
Q I want to ask you about how you might have known more about what stage of schizophrenia he was in.

A Sure.

Q Talking to the people he lived with would have helped?

A Yes.

Q But you did not talk to his parents?

A No.

Q Talking to the people he spent time with—his friends, would have helped?

A Yes.

Q But you did not talk to these people?

A No.

Q If you knew that the parents were extremely concerned about his actions, that would have been important to you?

A Yes.

Q And if they told you he was not the same person, that would be of importance to you?

A Certainly would.

Q If they told you he was socially withdrawing, that would have been important to you?

A Of course.

Q And if they told you he would sit in corners and just stare ahead, that would have been important to you?

A Yes, it would.

Q And if they told you he was deteriorating medically, that would certainly be important to you?

A Yes, sure.

Q These would have been signs that he was going through, the most severe stage, a prodromal stage?

A Some of the signs of it, yes.

Q Those would have been signs?

A Yes.

Q His brain would be starting to play tricks on him?

A Well, yes.

Q He was probably hallucinating?

A That is part of the symptomatology.

Q He was probably hallucinating?

A Yes.
Q He was probably delusional?
A Yes.
Q He probably entered an active stage of schizophrenia?
A At some time he did, because that's the way he was when I saw him.
Q So he probably entered an active stage of schizophrenia?
A Yes.
Q But you're not sure exactly when that would have been?
A No.
Q It would have helped you, of course, if you had a chance to talk, to say his parents with whom he was living?
A Yes.
Q And if they told you what was happening then, that would help?
A They would help, yes.
Q And if they told you that they became extremely concerned about him in late February, that would have been important to you?
A Certainly would.
Q And if you knew, that he was experiencing bizarre delusions, that would help you?
A Yes.
Q And if they told you he had a delusional fixation with being a CIA agent, that would help you?
A That would help me, yes.
Q If they told you he was hallucinating, that would have helped you?
A Yes.
Q And if they told you he was listening to voices, that would have helped you?
A Yes.
Q And if they told you all this was happening towards the last few days of February, that would have helped you?
A That would have been significant, yes.
Q So if they told you all this was happening towards the last few days of February, that would have significantly helped you?

A Yes.

Q And if the mother told you that she was so concerned, she called for medical assistance, that would have helped you?

A Yes.

Q But, again, you never took the time to talk to Robert Rice's parents?

A No.

Q So at the time you examined Robert Rice you did not know these important things?

A No.

Q So at the time you examined Robert Rice you did not know these significant things?

A No.

Q All of this information, which you did not have, supports the fact that he was in the active stage?

A Yes.

Q You did know he was in active state when you first talked to him?

A I talked to him in an active state, yes, at the beginning.

Q When you first examined him he was still in the active state?

A Yes.

Q You talked to him?

A I did.

Q And he talked to you?

A Yes.

Q And, of course, you heard what he said?

A Yes, I heard what he said.

Q And he heard what you said?

A Yes.

Q You asked him some questions?

A Yes.

Q He responded to your questions?

A For the most part, yes.

Q He responded to your questions?

A Yes.

Q He knew who you were?
A He did.
Q He knew where he was?
A Yes, he did.
Q He knew why he was there?
A Yes.
Q He knew the time?
A Yes.
Q He knew the date?
A Yes.
Q And at times, he could and did appear reasonably coherent?
A Yes.
Q At times, he would and did appear reasonably cooperative?
A Yes.
Q Is it fair to say, that even though he was in the active state of schizophrenia, he was oriented?
A Yes.
Q He was oriented in time? A time, date, person, and place, yes.
Q He was oriented in time?
A Yes.
Q In date?
A Yes.
Q In place?
A Yes.
Q And in person?
A Yes.
Q Because of that you could and did conclude that his orientation was correct?
A Yes.
Q Even though he was out of touch with reality?
A Yes.
Q By the way, that is not necessarily unusual?
A No.

Q Let me ask you some questions about the aircraft engineer you told us about yesterday.

A Yes.

Q This fellow had a rod going through his head?

A Yes.

Q This was a delusion?

A Yes.

Q His rod was connected to somebody out in California?

A Yes.

Q Wires were connected to an identical person somewhere in California?

A Right.

Q This person worked as an engineer.

A Yes.

Q As an aircraft engineer?

A Yes.

Q He could work with no problems?

A Yes.

Q It is probable that he could have gone through the active state of schizophrenia while he continued to work?

A With the presence of the delusion, yes.

Q People who saw him walk down the street, they would not know that he was delusional?

A No, they wouldn't.

Q They could not know he was in the active phase?

A No.

Q The people working with him would not know that he was delusional?

A No, they wouldn't necessarily know.

Q Then it is quite possible that somebody who is schizophrenic in the active state might still look good even to you?

A Yes, they may.

The Court: Did you hear that? Everybody hear that?

A Juror: There are times that he starts talking lower and I miss the last couple words of what he's saying.

The Court: Okay. So you have to keep your voice up at the end.
The Witness: Okay.
Mr. MacCarthy: I will keep mine up and maybe that will remind you.
Q If a seriously sick schizophrenia looked good to you, they would look good to others?
A Yes.
Q But they would still be delusional?
A Yes, indeed.
Q And they would still be psychotic?
A Yes, indeed.
Q I want to ask you some questions about your diagnosis of Robert Rice?
A Fine.
Q You diagnosed him as a chronic paranoid schizophrenic?
A Yes.
Q Paranoid is a type of schizophrenia?
A Yes.
Q Paranoid schizophrenia has certain essential features?
A Yes.
Q As a matter of fact, there are two essential features?
A Yes.
Q The first would be a preoccupation with one or more systemized delusions?
A Yes, sir.
A Yes.
Q The second one is a preoccupation with frequent auditory hallucinations related to a single theme?
A Yes.
Q I want to ask you some questions about the systematic delusions Robert Rice had in February of 1990?
A Fine.
Q He told you what his delusions were?
A Yeah. He told me what his delusions were.
Q He told you he was President of the United States?
A Yes.

Q You did not believe that, of course?

A No, it was a delusional material.

Q So you did not believe it?

A That's right.

Q This was a delusion he was going through?

A It was.

Q And he told you that he had his camera in his eye?

A Yes.

Q And that was a delusion he was going through?

A Sure.

Q He told you that he had lost his brain?

A Yes.

Q That was a delusion he was going though?

A Yes.

Q And he told you he was a CIA agent?

A Yes.

Q And that was a delusion he was going though?

A Yes.

Q I want to ask you some questions about what a delusional person might do, or how he might act, if he was to walk into a bank while suffering a delusion.

A Yes.

Q If he walked in as president, he would simply ask for all the money?

A He might do that if he was acting in keeping with the delusion, yes.

Q So if he walked in as president he would simply ask for all of the money?

A Yes.

Q If in his mind his delusion was not that of being the president, he might act differently?

A True.

Q He might act more in a covert way?

A He might, yes.

Q That would be in a way that he did not want people to know what he were doing?

A Yes.

Q He might act a bit secretive?

A Yes.

Q He would act secretive and in a covert way if that was consistent with his delusion?

A Yes.

Q To him that would be logic?

A That would be his logic, yes.

Q So to him it would be logic?

A Yes.

Q The delusion of being president, that's a relatively common delusion?

A Yes.

Q Another common delusion is the belief one is an FBI or CIA agent?

A That's a common theme.

Q Many people are delusional in believing that they are FBI agents?

A Yes.

Q And many people are delusional in believing that they are CIA agents?

A Yes.

Q I want to go back and ask you a few questions about paranoia?

A Sure.

Q Someone suffering from paranoia, thinks people are watching them?

A They might.

Q They think people are watching them?

A Yes.

Q Someone with paranoidal delusion who believes others are spying on him, would find it logical to act furtively?

A Yes, they might well do that.

Q They might act with stealth?

Q They might act mysteriously?

A Yes.
Q And fear?
A Yes.
Q The might act secretly?
A They might, yes.
Q The might act commandingly?
A They could.
Q So they might act commandingly?
A Yes.
Q Robert Rice told you that he was an agent for the CIA?
A He said he had been an agent for the CIA.
Q He told you he was an agent for the CIA?
A He said, "I was an agent for the CIA".
Q So he told you he was an agent for the CIA?
A Yes. Yes, in the past tense.
Q So he told you he was an agent for the CIA?
A Yes.
Q He did not tell you he was one when he was speaking to you?
A No, he didn't.
Q He told you he had been one in the past?
A Yes.
Q He also told you he was controlled by a computer?
A Yes.
Q That computer was in Washington?
A Yes.
Q Those delusions would affect his motive?
A Yes.
Q Those delusions would affect what he did?
A Yes.
Q I know want to ask you some questions about schizophrenia?
A Okay.
Q It is the most serious form of mental illness?
A It is a very serious form and one of the most debilitating there is.
Q It is the most serious form of mental illness?

A It can be. In its worst form it is a very serious disorder.
Q It's the most serious and debilitating of the mental illness?
A Yes.
Q In its active stage it is at its worst?
A Yes.
Q And yet you told us, few schizophrenic's require hospitalization?
A Yes, sir.
Q One to two percent?
A In that range, yes.
Q Now, I want to ask you some questions about what you did not see and what you did not read before you wrote your report. Do you understand?
A Yes.
Q You did not see or read Robert Rice's medical record?
A I didn't have any records on him.
Q You did not see or read Robert Rice's—medical records?
A No, I didn't have any records on him.
Q You did not have any record of his four hospitalizations for mental illness?
A I didn't.
Q You did not, see or read Dr. Adams examination results —
A No.
Q You did not read Dr. Adams report prepared for the Social Security Administration?
A No, I haven't seen that.
Q You did not know of, see, or read anything about his eleven outpatient visits for schizophrenia?
A No.
Q You did not know anything about his emergency room visits for schizophrenia?
A No.
Q You knew nothing about the record made by the Old Oak Hospital when Mrs. Rice called them on February 27, 1990?
A I didn't have any record of that, no.

Q So you knew nothing about it?
A That's right.
Q You wanted those things?
A I asked for them, yes.
Q You wanted them?
A Sorry?
Q You wanted them?
A I asked for them. You bet.
Q So you wanted them?
A Yes.
Q You knew they would be helpful?
A Yes.
Q You did not get them?
A I got some records long after I had left there.
Q You did not get that important information before you prepared your report?
A No. I didn't.
Q And so you did not see that critical information?
A No, I didn't.
Q It is fair to say that if you had this significant material, it would have been very helpful to you?
A Yes.
Q Your report was prepared without the benefit of that very helpful material?
A That's right.
Q Your report was prepared without the benefit of that significant material you wanted?
A Yes.
Q Now, I want to ask you about a few things you did not do. You understand?
A Yes.
Q You did not talk to Mrs. Rice?
A I did not.
Q You did not talk to Robert Rice's mother?

A I did not.
Q And you did not talk to Mr. Rice?
A No.
Q You did not talk to Robert Rice's father?
A No.
Q These were the two persons closest to him during his serious illness?
A Yes.
Q These were the two persons who knew more about him than anyone else?
A Yes.
Q These were the persons who were with him in late February of 1990?
A Yes. He was living at home with them at that time.
Q And these were the persons who knew what he was doing, what he was saying –
A Yes, sir.
Q – in late February of 1990?
A Yes, sir.
Q I want to ask you some questions about visits with Robert Rice from mid-May to mid-September.
A Sure.
Q You made notes of these visits?
A Yes.
Q You wrote down what he said?
A Yes.
Q That was important to you?
A Yes.
Q You wrote down your impressions?
A Yes.
Q That was important to you?
A Yes.
Q You no longer have those notes?
A No, sir.
Q You destroyed those notes?

A I threw them away.
Q By throwing them away you destroyed them?
A I guess so.
Q We have no way of checking those notes?
A No.
Q So we do not have a written record of exactly what he said?
A No.
Q Those important notes were shredded?
A They may well have been.
Q They were shredded?
A Yes.
Q So you did destroy these important notes?
A Yes.
Q After June 20th of 1990, anything he might have said to you is not recorded or written anyplace?
A Well, a hospital record was maintained and there may well be some entries in the hospital record.
Q After June 20th anything he said to you was shredded?
A Yes.
Q Robert Rice was sent to you for a medical diagnosis?
A He was sent to me for the purposes of determining answers to two questions.
Q He was sent to you for a medical diagnosis?
A To see if he had a mental illness, yes.
Q So, Robert Rice was sent to you for a medical diagnosis?
A Yes, sure.
Q You did a medical diagnosis of Robert Rice?
A Yes.
Q You did that because that is why he was sent to you?
A Yes.
Q Now, I want to ask you some questions about that medical diagnosis and the conclusions you reached. You understand?
A Yes.
Q You found that he had an illness?
A Yes.

Q You found that he had a mental illness?
A Yes
Q You found he had a serious mental illness?
A Yes.
Q He suffered from bizarre delusions?
A Yes.
Q He was hallucinatory?
A Yes.
Q He was schizophrenic?
A Yes.
Q He had paranoid type schizophrenic?
A Yes.
Q His disease was chronic?
A Yes.
Q He had a markedly disrupted thought processes?
A He certainly did.
Q He had a markedly disruptive thought processes?
A He certainly did.
Q So he had a markedly disruptive thought processes?
A Yes, sir.
Q He had been ravaged by schizophrenia?
A Yes.
Q The podromal stage of this terrible diagnosis?
A Yes.
Q The most active stage of this terrible diagnosis?
A Yes.
Q His mind would have been playing tricks on him?
A Yes.
Q Through all this he could and would appear normal to others?
A Yes.
Q He was a very sick young man?
A He was indeed.

The Court: We'll take a short break before the re-direct examination.
(Recess taken).

Cross-examination of the plaintiff's CEO and star witness in a civil case involving trade secrets, breach of contract, and fraud

by Michael A. Sherman
Partner, Alschuler Grossman Stein & Kahn, Santa Monica, California

Q Let's start out by going over the background you told the jury about on Monday morning in your direct examination by Mr. Mashenko. Okay?

A Okay.

Q You walked though your background from the age of 15 or 16 through the present?

A Yes.

Q In order, you were a miner?

A Yes.

Q A carpenter apprentice?

A Yes.

Q An insurance salesman?

A Yes.

Q A builder?

A Yes.

Q Then a banker?

A Yes.

Q You owned five banks?

A Yes.

Q And two savings and loan associations?

A Yes.

Q In Texas?

A Yes.

Q You eventually sold the banks?

A Yes.

Q You sold the banks in the early '70s?

A Yes.

Q You then got involved in real estate development?
A Yes.
Q In Monterey, California?
A Correct.
Q That development in Monterey didn't get started until sometime in the early to mid-1980s?
A That's correct.
Q We are missing about a five year block of time?
A Five years, yes.
Q You had to sell the banks?
A Yes, I sold the banks.
Q In the spring of 1973 you were convicted by a federal jury of three counts of mail fraud?
A Yes, I was.
Q You were sentenced to ten years in federal prison?
A Yes.
Q You were then ordered to surrender to federal marshals for imprisonment on May 13, 1974?
A Yes, I believe it was '74.
Q But you didn't surrender yourself?
A No.
Q Instead you became a fugitive from justice?
A Well, I didn't surrender.
Q You became a fugitive from justice?
A Yes.
Q You were a fugitive from justice for over two years?
A Approximately.
Q You were a fugitive from May, 1974 through July, 1976?
A Correct.
Q So you were a fugitive for over two years?
A Yes.
Q In July of 1976 you were arrested to Oceanside, California?
A Yes.

Q I want to ask you some questions about what you did during the over two years you were a fugitive?

A Yes.

Q You concealed your true identity from the public?

A Yes.

Q Your alias then, was Jack Bain?

Objection, Your Honor.

A Yes.

The Court: Overruled.

Q That was not your true name?

A Yes.

Q You lied about your true name?

A Yes.

Q You lied to help yourself?

A Yes.

Q You were finally brought to justice in September, 1976?

A Yes.

Q Before the federal court in Texas?

A Yes.

Q At that time you pled guilty to two more felonies?

A Yes.

Q The felony crime of bond jumping?

A Yes.

Q And the felony crime of bank fraud?

A Yes.

Q This time you were sentenced to 15 years in federal prison?

A Yes.

Q For these three felonies?

A Yes.

Q As a convicted felon you served five years in prison?

A Yes.

Q At Lompoc?

A Yes.

Continuation of a cross-examination of a snitch in a federal criminal case by Alison Siegler Assistant Federal Defender, Chicago

Q I want to ask you some questions about the night of September 21st when you went to Ms. Hernandez's house, you understand?

A Yes.

Q You ran into Maria Hernandez at a bar?

A Yes.

Q You'd been told she was involved with Oscar Gomez?

A Yes.

Q You knew she was a potential target of the investigation?

A Yes.

Q The agents had told you what to do if you made contact with a potential target?

A Yes.

Q You were supposed to let them know immediately?

A Yes.

Q You didn't follow those instructions?

A No.

Q Instead you went to Ms. Hernandez's house?

A Yes.

Q You went there for a reason?

A Yes.

Q You wanted to have sex?

A Yes.

Q You wanted to have sex with Ms. Hernandez?

A Yes.

Q You also wanted to have sex with Ms. Gonzalez?

A Yes.

Q You knew you were not supposed to have sex with a potential target?

A Yes.

Q Unfortunately for you, you did not have sex with Ms. Hernandez?
A No, I did not.
Q And you did not have sex with Ms. Gonzalez?
A No.
Q You did not have sex with anyone that night?
A No.
Q You did not have sex because the Cicero police came into the apartment?
A Yes.
Q You heard the police inside the apartment?
A Yes.
Q You didn't want to lose your deal with the government?
A Yes.
Q You didn't want to be prosecuted?
A Yes.
Q And of course you didn't want to stop getting paid?
A Well, I didn't want to be prosecuted.
Q You didn't want to stop getting paid?
A Right.
Q I want to ask you some questions about what happened when you talked to the agents about that night, you understand?
A Yes.
Q You talked to the agents on September 22?
A Yes.
Q It was the same day the Cicero police caught you at Ms. Hernandez's apartment?
A Yes.
Q You talked to Agent Smith that day?
A Yes.
Q You talked to Agent Jones?
A Yes.
Q Supervisor Walker was also there?
A Yes.
Q They wanted to know why you'd gone to Ms. Hernandez's apartment?

A Yes
Q You told them you went there for drinks?
A Yes.
Q That was a lie?
A Yes.
Q You specifically told the agents you did not go back to have sex?
A Yes.
Q And that was another lie?
A Yes.
Q You lied for a reason?
A Yes.
Q You lied to help yourself?
A Yes.
Q I want to talk about what you said happened that night and what really happened that night, you understand?
A Yes.
Q You 're now admitting that the *truth* is, you let Ms. Hernandez tie you up?
A Yes.
Q You were tied up for sexual purposes?
A Yes.
Q But when you first talked to the agents, you claimed you were tied up against your will?
A Yes.
Q That was a lie?
A Yes.
Q When you first talked to the police, you told them the women had a gun?
A Yes.
Q You gave the agents a pretty detailed description of what had happened with that gun?
A Yes.
Q You claimed Ms. Hernandez walked out of the kitchen?

A Yes.
Q And you claimed Ms. Hernandez returned moments later?
A Yes.
Q And you claimed she came back brandishing a gun?
A Yes.
Q And you said that she pointed that gun at you?
A Yes.
Q You said she then began questioning you about Oscar Gomez?
A Yes.
Q You said that was at gunpoint?
A Yes.
Q That was not the truth?
A No.
Q That was a lie?
A Yes.
Q You never saw an actual gun that night?
A Yes.
Q You also told the agents that Ms. Hernandez passed the gun to Ms. Gonzalez?
A Yes.
Q And you claimed Ms. Gonzalez kept the gun pointed at you?
A Yes.
Q You claimed that while Ms. Gonzalez had the gun pointing at you, Ms. Hernandez tied your hands?
A Yes.
Q But that never happened either?
A No.
Q That was a lie?
A Yes.
Q You also claimed you remembered what this so-called gun looked like?
A Yes.
Q You described this imaginary gun?
A Yes.

Q You described it several times?
A Yes.
Q You described it first to the Cicero police?
A Yes.
Q You described it in great detail?
A Yes.
Q You told them it was a revolver?
A Yes.
Q A small revolver?
A Yes.
Q And you said it was black?
A Yes.
Q That was a lie?
A Yes.
Q You later described this imaginary gun to the agents who interviewed you?
A Yes.
Q You said it was a handgun?
A Yes.
Q A revolver?
A Yes.
Q Black?
A Yes.
Q And again, that was a detailed description?
A Yes.
Q And again, that was a lie?
A Yes.
Q You never saw an actual gun?
A No.
Q But you made up a lot of little details about this nonexistent gun?
A Yes.
Q Those are the sorts of little details you knew the agents would rely on?

A Yes.

Q They're the same kind of little details you're providing here today?

A Yes.

Cross-examination of Detective John Davis in a federal criminal case by Steven R. Shanin Federal Defender (Chicago)

Q Before November 22, 1999, you had conducted surveillance on the 2700 block of Lewis?

A Yes, sir. I had.

Q Drive by surveillance?

A Yes, sir.

Q Not fixed surveillance?

A No, sir.

Q Never?

A Never.

Q To your knowledge, there was no fixed surveillance of this area by anyone else?

A Not that I'm aware of.

Q I want to ask you some questions about the beginning of your shift, on November 22, 1999?

A Okay

Q You started around 9:30 in the morning?

A Yes, sir.

Q You started out from your headquarters?

A Okay.

Q Your headquarters on Home Avenue?

A Yes.

Q You intended to set up a fixed surveillance of the 2700 block of Lewis?

A Yes, sir.

Q You took a video camera with you?

A No, sir.

Q A still camera?

A No, sir.

Q So it would be fair to say the pictures you showed us today were not taken at the time of the so-called surveillance?
A That's right, sir.
Q They were made up in preparation for this trial?
A I don't know. I suppose so.
Q They were made up in preparation for this trial?
A Yes.
Q You had binoculars with you?
A No, sir.
Q You had a tape recorder with you to record what actually happened?
A No, sir.
Q But you had paper and pens with you in case you had to make notes?
A We do carry paper and pens.
Q You had paper and pens with you?
A Yes, sir.
Q And you made notes?
A No.
Q You didn't make any notes?
A No.
Q You were with another officer?
A Yes, sir.
Q Officer Nance?
A Yes, sir.
Q Your partner?
A Yes, sir.
Q And the other officer drove?
A Yes.
Q To 2700 Lewis?
A Yes, sir.
Q Officer Nance dropped you off?
A Yes, sir.
Q About a block away?

A Yes, sir.
Q On the 2700 block of Pine?
A Yes, sir.
Q You set up an observation post there?
A Yes, sir.
Q You choose that location?
A Yes.
Q The building was vacant?
A Yes.
Q You set up on the porch?
A Yes, sir.
Q An outside porch?
A Yes, sir.
Q With an opening railing?
A Yes.
Q From your observation post you could see 2700 Lewis?
A Yes.
Q So it would be fair to say that if anyone was actually at 2700 Lewis, you could see them?
A Yes, sir.
Q And they could see you?
A I don't understand the question.
Q They could see you?
A So?
Q They could see you?
A I suppose. Yes.
Q And you could see where Officer Nance had set up?
A No.
Q But, you were in contact with him?
A No, not immediately.
Q So you cannot be sure what, if anything, Officer Nance saw?
A Yes.
Q Before you came here today, you review something?

A Yes.
Q For your story here today?
A Yeah. I had looked at my case report.
Q The one that you wrote.
A Yeah.
Q By yourself?
A Yeah.
Q From memory.
A Yeah.
Q You remembered the date of the arrest?
A Yeah.
Q And the time of the arrest?
A Yeah.
Q The weather conditions?
A Yeah.
Q It was pretty warm that day?
A I don't remember.
Q The *Tribune* said it was 57 degrees.
A Okay.
Q And you remembered all of the details you put into your report?
A Yeah.
Q And you put all of those details in your report?
A No.
Q You left out certain details?
A Yes, sir.
Q You did put all of the important details in your report?
A Yes, sir.
Q Where your observation post was?
A Yeah.
Q Where your partner was?
A Yeah.
Q The direction Mr. Don was walking when you first spotted him?
A Yeah.

Q What Mr. Don was supposedly carrying?
A Yeah.
Q In his hands?
A Yeah.
Q A bag?
A Yeah.
Q A plastic bag?
A Yeah.
Q I'm showing you Government Exhibit 4, a plastic bag. This is the plastic bag you say you saw Mr. Don carrying?
A Yes, sir.
Q The plastic bag you say you recovered at 2700 Lewis?
A Yes, sir.
Q Inside, you say were ten smaller plastic bags?
A Yes, sir.
Mr. Shanin: May I approach, Your Honor.
The Court: You may.
Q These are the small plastic bags you say were inside of the bag?
A Yes, sir.
Q And each of these bags is fastened closed with a strip of wide sticky tape?
A Yes, sir.
Q You also say you found a gun in the bag?
A Yes, sir. A loaded gun.
Q That would be the Government Exhibit Gun?
A Yes, sir.
Q The gun was loaded?
A Yes, sir.
Q With five metal bullets?
A Yes, sir.
Q It would be fair to say that someone loaded those metal bullets in the gun.
A Yes.
Mr. Shanin: May I approach, Your Honor.

The Court: Yes.

Q I'm showing you what has been introduced as Government Exhibit Gun. You are familiar with this type of gun?

A Yes, sir. It's a older type, thirty-eight caliber, five shot revolver.

Q Without actually loading it, would you please show to us how you would go about loading it.

A First you remove the center pin, like this. Then you take out the cylinder and put in the bullets.

Q So, holding the cylinder in one hand, you then take each bullets with the other hand and put in into the cylinder?

A Yes, sir.

Q And then you would take the cylinder and put it back into the gun?

A Yes, sir.

Q And then, holding the gun, you would screw the pin back?

A Yes.

Q Mr. Don's fingerprints were nowhere on the gun?

A No.

Q Now getting back to what you say you saw, when, as you say, Mr. Don laid down the bag?

A That's right.

Q Behind a tree?

A Yeah.

Q You say you saw the direction his first so-called customer was walking?

A Yeah.

Q. What the so-called customer looked like?

A Yeah.

Q What the so-called customer was wearing?

A Yeah. Yes.

Q What supposedly transpired between the so-called first customer and Mr. Don?

A Yeah.

Q You testified you thought it was a drug transaction?

A Yes, sir.

Q An illegal drug transaction?
A Yes.
Q It's illegal to buy drugs on the street?
A Yes, sir.
Q So it would be fair to say that the person was committing a crime?
A Yes, sir.
Q You arrested the person you thought was buying illegal drugs?
A No.
Q Your partner arrested him?
A No, sir.
Q But you found out who the so-called lawbreaker was so you could arrest him later?
A No.
Q You told us that you saw what you thought was a second drug transaction?
A Yes, sir.
Q Your reports, the ones you wrote out by yourself from your memory, mention this second so-called buyer.
A Yeah.
Q So it would be fair to say you saw what you thought to be a second drug transaction?
A Yeah.
Q You arrested the second so-called buyer?
A No.
Q I want to ask you some questions about Officer Nance, you understand?
A Yes.
Q He is still your partner?
A Yeah.
Q You're still together?
A Yeah, we still work together.
Q You drove here today?
A Yes.
Q With your partner?

A Sure.
Q You wrote up the arrest slip?
A Yeah.
Q From memory?
A Yes.
Q By yourself?
A Yeah.
Q You also wrote up the supplemental report?
A Yeah.
Q By yourself?
A Yeah.
Q And you wrote up the main police report?
A Yeah.
Q By yourself?
A Yeah.
Q And you reviewed copies of those reports you wrote before you told your story here today?
A Yeah.
Q And everything you told you here today is in those reports.
A Yeah.
Q And you brought those copies with you today?
A No.
Q You had them in the car with you?
A Yeah.
Q With you and Officer Nance?
A Yeah.
Q But you do not have those reports with you?
A No, sir.
Q You left them in the witness room across the hall?
A Yes.
Q Let me ask you some questions about what you did after you arrested Mr. Don, you understand?
A Yes.
Q You searched him?

A Yes, sir.
Q You found certain items on him?
A Yes, sir.
Q Sixty-three dollars in cash?
A Yes, sir.
Q Some keys?
A Yes, sir.
Q House keys?
A There were keys. I don't know what they were for.
Q There were no car keys?
A Yes.
Q No drugs?
A Not on him.
Q He had no drugs?
A Right.
Q No guns on him?
A The gun was with the drugs in his bag.
Q No guns were on him?
A No.
Q His bag? The one you say you saw him carrying?
A Yeah.
Q This shiny plastic bag with the Scotch tape across it?
A Yeah.
Q And you wrote out an inventory of those items you say you found?
A Yeah.
Q And that inventory you wrote has everything you say you found on Mr. Don?
A Yes.
Q The money?
A Yes.
Q Keys?
A Yes.
Q Mr. Don's clothing?

A Yes, sir.
Q His jacket?
A Yes, sir.
Q There's no hat listed?
A That's because he didn't have a hat on.
Q There's no hat listed?
A Right.
Q No scarf?
A He didn't have a scarf.
Q So it would be fair to say you inventoried all of his clothing?
A We did.
Q Again, when you say "we" you mean you?
A Yeah.
Q No gloves?
A No.
Mr. Shanin: Nothing further, Your Honor.

Cross-examination of a captain in an admiralty action
by James Mercante
Partner, Rubin, Fiorella & Friedman
New York, New York

Q We can agree that as a seaman, you expect your employer to provide you with a safe place to work?

A Yes, I do.

Q As a seaman, sometimes you are asked to go perform a task off of the vessel?

A Yes, I do.

Q To go aboard another vessel, as you did in this case?

A Yes.

Q You were directed by the master of your tug, the *Virginia*, to go aboard the crane barge?

A Yes, I was.

Q And you complied with that order?

A Yes, I did.

Q You tried to lift the heave chain off the bit?

A Yes.

Q But you couldn't do it?

A That's correct.

Q As a seaman, with your experience, you expected that the barge the master sent you to would be a safe place to work?

A Well, yes.

Q You had three- to five-foot seas?

A Yes.

Q Trying to left a heavy chain off a bit at the end of a barge was not a safe place to work on August 2nd, 1997?

A That's correct.

Q But you got sent off to the crane to move this chain?

A Yes.

Q Let me ask you some questions about handling lines, you understand?

A Yes.
Q Line handle is not a job for a captain with your experience?
A No.
Q Line hand is now a job for a captain with your experience?
A Well, I'm in the wheelhouse, but I know how to handle lines. I teach my deckhands how to do it.
Q You have an United States Coast Guard issued license?
A Yes.
Q You have had that license for a couple of decades?
A Thirty years, almost.
Q A captain steers the boat?
A Yes.
Q Let me ask you some questions about the duties and responsibilities of a captain?
A Yes.
Q A captain navigates?
A Yes.
Q A captain sets the course?
A Yes.
Q A captain sets the speed?
A Yes.
Q A captain may correct charts?
A Yes.
Q And a captain stands a watch?
A Yes.
Q On the *Virginia* you stood the 0600 to 1200 in the afternoon watch?
A Correct.
Q Then you stand the 6 p.m. watch to midnight?
A Correct.
Q Now, a deckhand is an unlicensed person?
A Yes.
Q They have no Coast Guard license?
A No.

Q They don't have a license to steer the boat?
A They don't have a license.
Q Or to navigate a boat?
A No.
Q Let me ask you some questions about the duties of a deckhand?
A Yes.
Q A deckhand's responsibility is to go on the deck?
A Yes.
Q That's why the call him a deckhand?
A Yes.
Q They handle lines?
A Yes.
Q They tie you up to the tug?
A Yes.
Q And let go of the tug?
A Yes.
Q And tie up a barge?
A Yes.
Q They take lines off a barge?
A Yes.
Q Those are things a deckhand does?
A Yes.
Q You were surprised when the master of the *Virginia* sent you on the deck of the barge to do the work of a deckhand?
A Well, in one way I was and in the other way I wasn't because he still needed his deckhand.
Q He needed his deckhand because the boat can't sail without a deckhand for your watch?
A Yes.
Q That deckhand would have accompanied you or would have went out instead of you?
A That's correct.
Q But because the boat was without a deckhand on your watch, you got stuck with this task?

A Yes.

Q A task that should have been done by a deckhand?

A Yes.

Q Let me ask you what the captain was asking you to do and what you understood.

A Yes.

Q He wasn't directing you to just hand rope/mooring lines?

A Correct.

Q He directed you to go handle a heavy chain?

A Yes.

Q Handling chain in parts a heavy chain is not a captain's job?

A No.

Q Or even a deckhand's job?

A No.

Q It's a job for a crane?

A A crane is what should be used to move a chain. You are not supposed to put your hand on a chain.

Q So it is a job for a crane?

A Yes.

Q You had seen this crane?

A Yes.

Q You saw it in Atlantic City?

A Yes.

Q It is the crane that's in the picture?

Mr. Mercante: May I approach, Your Honor?

The Court: Go ahead.

Q You know what this is?

A Yes. A picture of the crane.

Q This is the crane barge?

A That's correct.

Q We can see the full extent of the crane arm?

A That's correct.

Q Its operator took the chain off the bit?

A That's correct.

Q And that was when it was in calm conditions?
A Yes.
Q Alongside a dock?
A Yes.
Q With no seas?
A Yes.
Q And no wind in Atlantic City?
A Yes.
Q This was really not a job for a man?
A Yes.
Q It's a job for a crane?
A Well, the crane was supposed to take it off, as far as I know.
Q It is a job for a crane?
A Yes.
Q The crane was supposed to take off the chain from the bit?
A Yes.
Q This was supposed to be done in calm waters?
A Yes.
Q In Moriches Inlet?
A Yes.
Q In calm waters?
A Yes.
Q With no wind?
A Yes.
Q And no seas?
A Yes.
Q Just like it was done in Atlantic City?
A That's correct.
A No.
Q Let me ask you about the heavy chain that Mr. Moore struggled with to bring over to the jury box?
A Yes.
Q That is the chain they expected you and the tugboat *Montana* personnel to remove from that bit?

A Yes.
Q While at sea?
A Yes.
Q While under way?
A Yes.
Q And with three- to five-foot sea conditions?
A Yes.
Q And you knew that that task was going to be impossible?
A Yes, I did.
Q And you thought that to yourself before you went on the crane?
A Yes.
Q But, as a good seaman with 30 years experience, you followed Captain Less's order?
A. Yes.
Q Captain Less is the captain of the *Virginia*?
A Yes.
Q You followed his orders?
A Yes.
Q You went on that crane?
A Yes; he is the master.
Q Before going on the crane after being order to do so by Captain Less you told had to? (Did not understand his rewrite.)
A Yes.
Q You had told him you thought it was getting kind of rough to break this tow?
A Yes, I did.
Q And you told him that you weren't happy with the situation?
A Yes, I did.
Q But he sent you anyway?
A Yes, he did.
Q He took the tug *Virginia* around to the barge?
A Yes.
Q He dropped you off on the crane?
A Yes.

Q Without a deckhand?
A No deckhand.
Q He expected you to do this with your hands?
A Yes.
Q You had no tools?
A That's right.
Q The crane barge has a rack for chains?
A Yes.
Q There were plenty of chains on the barge?
A Yes.
Q And there are plenty of shackles on this barge?
A Yes.
Q Huge shackles?
A Yes.
Q Attached to the chain?
A Yes.
Q And there is the bit on this barge?
A Yes.
Q There is all sorts of equipment on the barge?
A Yes.
Q Let me ask you about the typical equipment on a tugboat?
A Yes.
Q This type of chain rack is not typical equipment?
A That's correct.
Q But it's technical equipment for a crane barge?
A Yes.
Q So you would think if there was any equipment to lift this chain from between two vessels, the barge would have that equipment?
A Yes.
Q But it wasn't there?
A I didn't see it.
Q It was not there?
A Right.

Q. There was no chain hook?
A I didn't see any.
Q There was no chain hook?
A No.
Q This crane barge also has an equipment container?
A Yes, it does.
Q This is where they keep miscellaneous equipment?
A Yes.
Q They did not give you a key to that?
A No.
Q You knew what was in it?
A I know it was locked.
Q You knew what was in it?
A Yes.
Q But is was locked?
A Yes.
Q The captain send you on this barge without a key to the equipment locker?
A That's correct.
Q And he sent you on that barge without a chain hook?
A Yes.
Q And he sent you on that barge without a torch?
A I didn't see any torch.
Q He sent you on the barge without a hacksaw?
A I didn't see any hacksaw.
Q He sent you on the barge with only your two hands?
A Yes.
Q And he sent you on that barge without a torch?
A I didn't see any torch.
Q he sent you on the barge without a hacksaw?
A I didn't see any hacksaw.
Q He sent you on the barge with only your two hands?
A Yes.

Q You were smart enough to bring gloves?
A Yes.
Q The captain didn't give you gloves?
A I had my own gloves just in case.
Q The captain did give you gloves?
A No.
Q Now, you made some attempts by yourself?
A Yes, I did.
Q You tried twice?
A Yes.
Q While you were trying ways the captain of the *Montana* was looking down from the wheelhouse at you?
A Yes.
Q He saw you struggling?
A Well, he might have, I don't remember at that point.
Q He was in the wheelhouse?
A Oh, yes.
Q He saw you struggling?
A Yes.

Continuation of a cross-examination of a county sheriff in a federal criminal case by Heather E. Williams Assistant Federal Defender Tucson, Arizona

Q You never asked Mr. Gonzales the names of his family members?

A No, I don't recall that.

Q You did not ask him if he knew any family members of the other people in the group?

A No.

Q On direct examination you explained some of your background, I would like to ask you some questions about that, you understand?

A Yes.

Q You are 27 years old?

A Yes.

Q And you were just promoted to sergeant last June?

A Yes.

Q Before that you were a detective?

A Yes.

Q For three years?

A Yes.

Q So you were made a detective when you were about 24?

A More or less, yes.

Q And you have been with the County Sheriff's Office for a total of eight years?

A Yes.

Q That means you started when you were 19?

A Yes.

Q You were promoted very quickly?

A Yes.
Q You have aspirations to work in federal law enforcement?
A Yes.
Q You are going to school?
A Yes, to college.
Q To Puma College?
A Yes.
Q You are studying criminal justice?
A Yes.
Q Now I want to ask you about the report you wrote in this case, you understand?
A Yes.
Q That was part of your duties in the investigation?
A Yes.
Q You did this as a member of the county sheriff's office?
A Yes.
Ms. Williams: Your Honor, may I show the witness Defense Exhibit 510?
The Court: Yes you may.
Q You know what this is?
A Yes.
Q It is a copy of your department report?
A Yes.
Q It describes what you did on June 3rd, 1998?
A Yes.
Q You received a call to go to Potter Canyon about 3:25 in the morning?
A Yes.
Q And got there about an hour later?
A Yes.
Q You arrived with other members of the sheriff's office?
A Yes.
Q Including Sergeant Paul Ramirez?
A Correct.

Q And Detective Ralph Fine?
A Yes.
Q And Detective Paul Ramirez who is different from the Sergeant Paul Ramirez?
A Yes.
Q And Ray James met you there?
A Correct.
Q And he is from the police department?
A Correct.
Q When you arrived, you found out that an alien had been arrested?
A Yes.
Q You saw the person who was arrested?
A Yes.
Q Detective Fine took a picture of him?
A Yes.
Q You talked to him?
A Informational questions, yes.
Q So you talked to him?
A Yes.
Q And you found he was an undocumented alien?
A Yes.
Q Officer James showed you and Detective Fine around the scene?
A Yes.
Q Then the FBI arrived about a quarter to six in the morning?
A Yes.
Q And then you showed the FBI agents around the scene?
A Yes.
Q That was about 5:55?
A Yes.
Q You stayed there until a little bit after 7?
A Yes.
Q Then you left with Jay Harrison?
A Correct.

Q And he is with the FBI?
A Yes.
Q As you left the canyon area, you followed behind two border patrol cars?
A I don't recall the exact number of vehicles.
Q But you did follow more than one car?
A Yes.
Q They were ahead of you?
A Yes.
Q And they were border patrol?
A Yes.
Q You saw the front border patrol car stop?
A Yes.
Q They stopped a man?
A Yes.
Q That was Michael Gonzalez?
A Yes.
Q I want to ask you some questions about your training in writing police reports?
A Yes.
Q It is an important part of your job?
A Yes.
Q You know they need to be completed?
A As much as possible, yes.
Q They must include all the details?
A Well, it is—I am pretty sure we leave out details, but try to write as much as we can.
Q Because you are only human?
A Correct.
Q And you can't always remember everything?
A Right.
Q But one of the reasons you write the reports is so in the future you will be able to recall as much as possible?
A Yes.

Q And to help you to do that you include times in your report?
A Correct.
Q And you have done that in this report?
A Yes.
Q You do that so others can use the report for further investigation?
A Right.
Q And you do that so you can refresh your memory when it comes time to testify or talk with people about the case?
A Yes.
Q Now, you told us that as this time you prepared this report you were a part of the homicide assault unit?
A Yes.
Q As a detective with that unit, you would have cause to interview witnesses?
A Yes.
Q And sometimes victims?
A Yes.
Q And in your report, you would summarize what was told you?
A Yes.
Q And you would include what they were able to tell you?
A Yes.
Q You would include descriptions in the report?
A Yes.
Q Descriptions of a suspect?
A Yes.
Q And you would try to get a name if they knew the name?
A Yes.
Q Sometimes they wouldn't know the name?
A Yes.
Q And sometimes they would only know a first name?
A Yes.
Q And sometimes they might only know a nickname?
A Yes.

Q Sometimes they wouldn't know the person's address?
A Yes.
Q But sometimes they would be able to give you directions on how to get to where the person lived?
A Yes.
Q They would try to give you an idea about the person's height?
A Yes.
Q And they would give you an idea about weight of the person?
A Yes.
Q And they would give you the person's body build?
A Yes.
Q And they would describe hair color?
A Yes.
Q They would tell you the kind of clothing the person had on?
A Yes.
Q And you and other officers would use this description and all this information to try to find the suspect?
A Yes.
Q And while it might not be as complete as you would like, it wouldn't stop you from continuing your investigating?
A Right.
Q Now, when you interview a suspect, you try and include information about the interview with the suspect in your report, also, correct?
A Yes.
Q And that would include information about Miranda rights?
A Yes.
Q That is an important matter that might be an issue at trial?
A Yes.
Q And you would include details about what had happened—what the suspect said happened?
A Right.
Q In your practice with the sheriff's office, you normally tape record interview with suspects?

A Yes.
Q And you normally tape record interviews with witnesses?
A Yes.
Q And you normally tape record interviews with victims?
A Yes.
Q And that is because tape recordings are the most accurate way to preserve exactly what was said?
A Yes.
Q The tape will preserve accurately what questions you asked?
A Yes.
Q And the tone of voice that you use?
A Yes.
Q And it will preserve what is told to you in return?
A Yes.
Q Now, I want to ask you some specific questions about your report in this case?
A Yes.
Q Your report is two pages?
A Correct.
Q Two typewritten pages?
A Yes.
Q You participated in this investigation for over 15 hours on June the 3rd?
A Yes.
Q Yet all of the details in your 14-hour investigation are in that two-page report?
A Yes.
Q Your report mentions FBI reports?
A Yes.
Q You were referring to the three interviews you did with the FBI?
A Yes.
Q One of those is the interview done by Agent McIntyre?
A Correct.
Q And that was the interview of Sam Hall?

A Yes.
Q And one of those interviews was the 11:30 interview of Mr. Gonzales?
A Yes.
Q That was the one where you were with Agent Galvan?
A Yes.
Q And you were referring to the afternoon interview with Mr. Galvan?
A Correct?
Q Now, I would like to talk a little bit about Mr. Hall's interview?
A Yes.
Q Your report says "see Case Agent James McIntyre PFD 302 form from the FBI reference interview with Border Patrol Agent Sam Hall"?
A Yes.
Q You didn't summarize in your report what was said during that interview?
A No.
Q You intended to have people refer to Agent McIntrye's report?
A Yes.
Q And if you needed to, you, yourself, could review Agent McIntyre's report?
A Right.
Q But that interview was not taped?
A No.
Q You wrote notes of what was said during that interview?
A Yes.
Q Your notes include two pages?
A Yes.
Q In that interview, Mr. Gonzales told you there were five back-packers?
A Yes.
Q Now, I would like to ask you some questions about the first interview you had with Mr. Gonzales.
A Okay.

Q Your report "see Agent Galvan's PFD 302 form reference the details of the interview with Gonzales"?

A Yes.

Q And again you didn't summarize the interview in your report?

A Right.

Q You have already talked about how in coming to court today you use Agent Galvan's report to help you refresh your memory?

A Yes.

Q You even referred to his handwritten notes of the interview to help you refresh your memory?

A Yes.

Q That interview with Mr. Gonzales was not taped?

A No.

Q But you wrote notes about what was said during the interview?

A Yes.

Q Those notes are two pages and one line on the third page?

A Yes.

Q The three pages actually include the second interview?

A Right.

Q Of Mr. Gonzales?

A Right.

Q So the very first interview, is two pages and one line on to the third page?

A Yes.

Q During the second interview, you went back and added information you had written during the first interview?

A Right.

Q The interview you and Agent Galvan conducted of Mr. Gonzales lasted one hour and a half?

A Yes.

Q Mr. Galvan handled the interview for the first 30 to 45 minutes?

A Yes.

Q You had a chance to hear Mr. Galvan's Spanish?

A Yes.

Q You commented that it was more formal than the kind of Spanish you use?
A Yes.
Q It appeared to you that Mr. Gonzales had no problems understanding Mr. Galvan?
A No problems.
Q. And you felt Mr. Galvan was able to understand Mr. Gonzales?
A Yes.
Q But it seemed like the interview wasn't really going anywhere?
A Yes.
Q You took over the interview?
A Yes.
Q You felt you would have a better rapport with Mr. Gonzales?
A Yes.
Q Your were younger and used street Spanish?
A Yes.
Q Now, while you questioned Mr. Gonzales, you weren't writing?
A Right.
Q You were concentrating more on your questions?
A Yes.
Q And his body language?
A Yes.
Q And his answers?
A Yes.
Q You also saw that Agent Galvan was taking notes?
A Yes.
Q You knew you would be able to rely on those to refresh your memory in the future?
A Yes.
Q You recently reviewed Mr. Galvan's notes?
A Yes, about two days ago.
Q Agent Galvan's notes are accurate as per your recall?
A Yes.

Q Those are the notes you noted you reviewed to refresh your memory?
A Yes.
Q That report is two and a half pages?
A Yes.
Q. And those are typewritten pages?
A Yes.
Q This report basically summarizes the answers?
A Yes.
Q But it does not really reflect all the questions that were asked?
A Right.
Q Except for that, this report seems to be accurate?
A Yes.
Q I would like to talk with you a little bit about the Miranda warnings you were present for.
A Yes.
Q It was Agent Galvan who first read them to Mr. Gonzales.
A. Yes.
Q He read them off a sheet of paper?
A Yes.
Q And he read them in Spanish?
A Correct.
Q After he read the rights he then handed the form to Mr. Gonzales?
A Correct.
Q And Mr. Gonzales looked it over?
A Yes.
Q And then Agent Galvan asked Mr. Gonzales if he understood those rights?
A Yes.
Q Mr. Gonzales nodded his head?
A Yes.
Q He answered yes in Spanish?
A Yes.

Q And then Agent Galvan asked Mr. Gonzales to sign the form where he understood his rights?
A Correct.
Q And Mr. Gonzales did sign it?
A Yes.
Q He also dated it?
A Yes.
Q He also wrote in the location?
A Correct.
Q Then Agent Galvan signed it?
A Yes.
Q Then you signed it also?
A Correct.
Q That is not where the forms ends?
A No.
Q I would like to talk about the next section, the waiver section?
A Okay.
Q In English the heading of that section says "waiver"?
A Yes.
Q On the form that was handed to Mr. Gonzales that was in Spanish?
A Yes.
Q That is where the suspect signing the form gives up all those rights at the beginning of the form?
A Yes.
Q And it is the place where the suspect agrees to go ahead and talk to you?
A Yes.
Q But they must sign that if they agree to give up all those rights?
A Yes.
Q But there is no signature on this form?
A No, there isn't.
Q There is no signature on the waiver section?
A Correct.

Q And there is no date on the waiver section?

A Correct.

Q I would like to talk with you about the descriptions that Mr. Gonzales gave you during the first interview?

A Okay.

Q On page four of your notes, you wrote the descriptions that were given to you during the first interview?

A Yes.

Q I am going to hand you a black marker, and if you could copy from your notes the description of Ernesto?

A Yes.

Q You have written Ernesto, male, five foot four inches, 22 years old, skinny, dark complexion, brown pants, gray sweat shirt, and white tennis shoes?

A Correct.

Q You have something written before the brown pant description?

A Yes.

Q It says "loose"?

A Yes.

Q Could you kind of wedge that in there, please.

A (Witness complies.)

Q And I think you also have in here something that says "cholo-type"?

A Yes.

Q That was written during the first interview?

A Yes.

Q If you could please add that.

A (Witness complies.)

Q The loose brown pants type of attire, a cholo-type, that a gangster-type look?

A Yes.

Q It is a kind of style of clothes that has been associated with gangsters?

A Yes.

Q You also have a description of that on your handwritten notes?

A That is correct.
Q That was added in the second interview?
A Yes.
Q The next person listed is a John?
A Yes.
Q The name John added in the second interview?
A Yes.
Q Could you write the description then of the second person as you got it in the first interview?
A Yes.
Q Thank you.
A (Witness complies.)
Q Now, to write this you refer to Agent Galvan's report and your notes, correct?
A Yes.
Q You have written male known as El Smack, short, five foot one inch, fat, about 22 years old, dark pants, dark blue jacket?
A Yes.
Q Agent Galvan's report where you took this from, refers to this person as Gordo?
A Yes.
Q Write that in, also? And Gordo cannot just be a description, it can also be a nickname?
A Yes.
Q You have also written in your report a description of the third person, Pepe?
A Yes.
Q Please write the summary of that from the first interview.
A Yes.
(Witness complies.)
Q And you have written Pepe, 26 to 27 years old, five foot nine inches, disheveled short hair, thin build, dark complexion?
A Yes.
Q And that basically summaries what you have in your notes?
A Summarized, yes.

Q You mentioned a translation?

A Yes.

Q You put in your notes that word “moreno”?

A Yes.

Q That would mean medium complexion?

A Yes.

Q Not dark complexion?

A Medium.

Q There was some discussion yesterday about the first interview when Michael told you certain things happened at certain times, and I would like to talk with you about that.

A Okay.

Q In your notes you wrote 4 p.m. on page four.

A Yes.

Q And that is followed by “money, took it away.”

A Yes.

Q But those two aren’t really connected together?

A No.

Q Yesterday you told us Mr. Gonzales said he met the three others on June the 2nd about 3 to 4 in the afternoon?

A Yes.

Q And that was at La United?

A Yes.

Q Then later on, on that same page, you have written 8 p.m., night?

A Yes.

Q And that is followed by $400?

A Yes.

Q Then “black bag” with the NI in parenthesis?

A Yes.

Q You told us that that is when they got together to actually start their walk to the border?

A Yes.

Q It is possible then that at 3 to 4 in the afternoon they got together, the offer was made, they made the arrangements then to meet later that night to actually do the walking?

A Yes that is possible.

Q You remember that $400 was offered to cross illegally into the United States?

A To carry the marijuana load, yes.

Q To bring backpacks and cross illegally into the United States?

A Yes.

Q And then having made those arrangements, they got together again that night?

A Yes.

Q And that they were taken by a pickup truck to an area outside of the town?

A Yes.

Q To a place of Nuevo Rico.

A Correct.

Q And the bags were already in the truck?

A Yes.

Q And there were four bags there?

A Yes.

Q And that each person in the group got a bag?

A Yes.

Q And then they started walking north?

A Yes.

Q And they walked for about three hours in Mexico until they got to the United States border?

A Approximately, yes.

Q And then after they crossed the border, they walked for another two hours before the saw the border patrol?

A Border patrol, yes.

Q So you understand that they had walked a total of about five hours?

A Approximately.

Q I would like to talk a little bit about the description of the gun, okay?
A Yes.
Q Now, in your notes regarding the gun, you only wrote after the word "Chi Chi" .38 revolver?
A Right.
Q You didn't write in there anything about when Michael first knew about it?
A I didn't.
Q Not in your notes?

A Not in my notes.
Q And nothing about Michael touching it in your notes?
A Right.
Q Now, do you remember, Mr. Gonzales saying that the person in the lead had a gun?
A Yes.
Q And that Chi Chi was the one that had the gun?
A Yes.
Q And that Michael had handled the gun earlier?
A Yes.
Q But he didn't put his finger on the trigger?
A Correct.
Q And you remember him also saying he was not the shooter?
A Yes.
Q And that he was willing to take a paraffin test?
A Yes.
Q Now, you stated that Michael first saw the gun when they got together on June the 2nd?
A Correct.
Q Now, Mr. Gonzales explained to you that during their walk, the group had several rest and water breaks?
A Correct.
Q He explained to you that it was during one of those water breaks that he saw Chi Chi had a gun?

A Yes.
Q I would like to talk about what you told us yesterday about what Michael said as to why he though Chi Chi had a gun?
A Okay.
Q Now, yesterday you said that Mr. Gonzales thought that he had a gun because of ganadores?
A Correct.
Q And you interpreted that as being people who might win over the drugs from them?
A Yes.
Q But there is nothing in your notes about that?
A Right.
Q I would like to talk about the description you received about the bags?
A Yes.
Q Your notes refer to Mr. Gonzales' bag in two separate places?
A Yes.
Q On the first page of the first interview, you wrote black bag and then NI in parenthesis?
A Yes.
Q And then on the second page you wrote "white in color"?
A Correct.
Q You are telling us that that was the way to remind you that his bag had a Nike sign on it?
A Yes.
Q And you understood that to be that Nike swoosh?
A Nike sign.
Q The thing that looks like the wave, you described it?
A Right.
Q But you are not a good artist, so you didn't draw a picture of it?
A Right.
Q And the NI on the first page and the big N on the second page are your shorthand for Nike?
A Yes.

Q And that was to remind you?

A Yes.

Q I would like for you to refer to page 6 of your notes, please. On page 6, you wrote the description of three ball caps?

A Yes.

Q Those descriptions came from ball caps that were found at the scene?

A Yes.

Q One of the caps was a Nike cap?

A Yes.

Q And you wrote out the word "Nike," N-I-K-E?

A Right.

Q Now, at some point in the interview, before you started taking over the questioning, you asked Mr. Gonzales to pull up his shirt?

A Yes.

Q And that was so you could see if he had the marks that are typical of somebody backpacking drugs?

A Right.

Q He seemed shocked by that?

A Yes.

Q I would like to talk with you about the nicknames that were used, you understand?

A Yes.

Q You have said the nickname Chi Chi means an infant or a small child?

A Yes.

Q You have also said the nickname Gordo means somebody who is fat?

A Yes.

Q I would like to talk a little bit now about the second interview where you were present with Agent Galvin.

A Yes.

Q Now, apparently the goal of this interview was to see if you could get any better information?

A Right.

Q Better names?

A Correct.

Q Addresses in Mexico?

A Yes.

Q And better descriptions of the people?

A Yes.

Q And you said yesterday that is because you were running out of time?

A Yes.

Cross-examination of a securities trading firm auditor by John Buckley, Ungaretti & Harris, Chicago, Illinois

Q You signed an affidavit detailing the money paid to Mr. Black?
A Yes.
Q He was the CEO?
A Yes.
Q This money included payment for services?
A Yes.
Q Pay for loan payments?
A Yes.
Q And pay for the reserve fund?
A Yeah.
Q In your affidavit you have three buckets?
A Yes.
Q The first bucket is compensation for services as CEO?
A Yes.
Q As president?
A Yes.
Q As sales manager?
A Yes.
Q And as Chairman of the Board?
A Yes.
Q Your intent was to make sure that the payment reflected the pay for services in each one of the positions that Mr. Black held during that four-year tenure?
A I believe—yes.
Q So bucket No. 1 reflects compensation for services?
A Yes.
Q Now, I want to ask you some questions about your bucket No. 2, you understand?
A Yes.
Q Bucket No. 2 is debt service bonuses?

A Yes.

Q There were a number of different debt service bonuses?

A Yes.

Q Those debt services bonuses included minimum debt payment bonuses?

A Yes.

Q They included excess cash flow bonuses?

A Yes.

Q There were also interest payment bonuses during this period of time when the principal payments were being paid out of the reserve?

A Yes.

Q And all of these debt bonuses are grossed up for taxes?

A Yes.

Q The debt bonus takes care of not only the payment he has to make, but also any tax liability he would have?

A Yes.

Q In addition, there are CEO reserve bonuses on top of all that?

A Yes.

Q And those are bonuses that go to the reserve fund?

A Yes.

Q That reserve fund was not a company fund?

A No.

Q It's a personal account in Mr. Black's name?

A Yes.

Q In fact, he paid personal income taxes on the amount that went into the reserve fund?

A Yes.

Q There was no requirement that he give any of those monies back?

A No.

Q There was no limitation on how Mr. Black spent money in the reserve account?

A No.

Q There was no way to stop him from writing a check from the reserve account?

A He would have to sign the check.
Q He could go to the bank and withdraw money?
A If he knew what bank it was at.
Q He knew what bank it was at?
A Maybe.
Q He knew what bank it was at?
A Yes.
Q Now, these different bonuses were paid at different times?
OPPOSING COUNSEL Mr. Hill: Objection to form.
JUDGE: Overruled.
Q They were paid at different times?
A Yeah.
Q The minimum debt bonus was paid in monthly installments in 1999?
A Yes.
Q And at the time you were paying these principal and interest payments, you were also grossing them up for taxes?
A I'm not sure if we did in '00 because of the—yeah, we did.
Q So you would have an additional bonus called a tax bonus?
A Yes.
Q In addition to that you had an excess cash flow bonus?
A Yes.
Q And the excess cash flow bonus, in summary fashion, was approximately 50 percent of the net revenue of the firm twice a year?
A Yes.
Q Now, in addition, you have called this annual take-home bonus a gross bonus?
A I believe our comptroller might have referred to that.
Q So you called it a gross bonus?
A Yes.
Q No one else at The Brown Companies gets a minium debt bonus?
A No.

Q Minority shareholders at The Brown Companies did not get a minimum debt bonus?

A No.

Q Other employees at The Brown Companies did not get a minimum debt bonus?

A No.

Q Minority shareholders at The Brown Companies did not get a reserve bonus?

A No.

Q No employees at The Brown Companies got a reserve bonus?

A No.

Q Nobody associated with The Brown Companies ever got an excess cash flow bonus other than Mr. Black?

A No.

Q No workplace evaluation of Mr. Black's performance, job responsibilities and work as an employee was undertaken and completed before you cut him the check on December 31st, 1999?

A Yes.

Q Bonuses for employees in '99 were distributed in January of 2007?

A Yes.

Q Mr. Black was treated differently?

A Yes.

Q It was given to him in December of 1999?

A Yes.

Q You would agree that most employees at The Black Companies had their reviews before bonuses were handed out to them?

A Yes.

Q Mr. Black was an exception to that rule?

A Yes.

Index

H

I

K

L

M

N

O

P

S